AF265113

Diary of a Dancin' Girl

Written by
Patricia Halliday-Kuklenski

Edited by
Allene Halliday

2024

ISBN: 978-0-578-62198-2

Library of Congress Control Number: 2023923473

Copy Editor: Angela Jones
Cover Design: Kathy Wrobleski ~ The Print Guys/B&B Printing
Book Design: Cat Wallace ~ www.wordworthymedia.com

*Dedicated to Jat and Betty Herod
and all the Manhattan Models*

Roger's Mom was in. We waited
around club until 2:30 A.M.
because Pen had an appointment
call with Kent. We were hoping
it would be the Fourteen then
but no such luck. He said they'd
left for L.A. All but Ken are
married anyway. Mrs. Herod
said I was getting lazy about
keeping my stomach in. Got
to bed at 4:00.
Sun. Aug. 7 — Got up at 10:30 &
sunbathed & sewed on beach &
finished "Silver Chalice." Not a
very big crowd tonight. Bunny
drove us home & got borrowed
the record player. Girls went
out on dates & got home at
3:30. We got to bed at 4:00.
Mon. Aug. 8 — Got up at 11:00.
Did washing, sewing, shopping & went
to a party at Mr. Waller's Summer
place. It's a little cottage finished
inside with knotty pine & with
trimmings of bearskins, etc. It's
on a hill overlooking a beautiful
valley of farmland which he owns.
We had a ham dinner with

A page from Pat's journal

Prologue

By Allene Halliday

The Manhattan Cocktail Review

It was unique in its time. Appearing between the demise of vaudeville and the birth of television entertainment, this miniature revue followed the successful formula of New York City's supersize revues: attractive chorus girls in captivating costumes, clever comedy sketches, novelty acts, song and dance specialties, and a bit of culture thrown in to round out the program.

Since there were only six people in the troupe this was quite an achievement! The name, Manhattan Cocktail Revue, with its ring of sophistication, belied the fact that most of the group had never been anywhere near New York, much less Manhattan Island. No matter! Crisscrossing the nation on two-lane highways in a Pontiac station wagon pulling a trailer filled with costumes, music, and props, they performed in the nightclubs of small cities and towns fifty weeks out of the year.

Betty Bryant, who'd grown up entertaining on her family's Ohio River showboat, and her husband, Jat Herod, who'd been a child protégé violinist (until he grew up) started the revue in Honolulu, Hawaii, in 1947 when they hired a sister act, The Gaylords.

Using special arrangements, the two girls sang old tunes in close harmony. And they could dance! With the sisters, the Herods created a complete show of jokes, songs, puppets, skits, music, and dancing. This small, lively entertainment package became the first Manhattan Cocktail Revue. The format was so successful, the show soon added two more dancers with their own individual specialty routines. Now the revue could open and close its shows by presenting small-scale production numbers with Jat and Betty fronting their chorus line of four good-looking, talented dancers. The troupe became the envy of other acts. None could duplicate it. The Herods were geniuses in performance and business.

The show's publicity boasted that it could run from twenty

minutes to twenty hours without repeating a number. Technically that was true; there were tons of routines, tons of costumes, and tons of music. However, most of these were stored in several locations across the country: Phoenix in the West, Chicago in the Midwest, and Atlanta in the South. When the Herods changed shows, they scheduled a stopover at one of these spots to trade the current show's paraphernalia for that of the new production's. Conveniently, their booking agents were also located in these cities. When necessary, the agents could be relied upon to ship the needed accouterments wherever the troupe was appearing for an extended period of time, such as Hawaii for four months!

During this era, nightclubs had house bands, so it wasn't necessary for acts to travel with musicians of their own. Nevertheless, it was handy having an accomplished violinist heading our troupe. Jat took charge of band rehearsals and directed our performances from the bandstand. His musical virtuosity provided the show's cultural interlude. In addition, he handled the bookings and acted as emcee, singer, and stand-up comedian.

Betty was an equally integral component of the show's success. As choreographer, costume designer, chief seamstress, comedienne, lead dancer, and "hoofer" extraordinaire, Betty's versatility and creativity were the backbone of the show. The chorus routines she devised ranged from graceful hulas and charming waltzes to high-kicking cancans and Charlestons.

The chorines, known as the Manhattan Models, contributed a variety of specialties to the mix. Acrobatics. Individual song and dance. Toe-tap. A couple of popular specialty numbers, an energetic Cossack routine, and the venerable Mexican Hat Dance were inherited from dancers who retired from the show. These were performed by new recruits until they had developed their own specialties.

Thanks to Jat's onstage comedy patter between numbers along with well-timed quick costume changes by the dancers backstage, the fast-paced performances ran smoothly.

The chorus girls were well paid. In return, the Herods required them to behave like professionals both on and off the stage. When the Manhattan Models walked into a club, they were to be in full makeup, wearing attractive cocktail dresses, tasteful jewelry, and preferably fur stoles as wraps. They were also to look like "The Show!" by dressing well and behaving with decorum when they were shopping or in a restaurant because, in the small cities or towns where they worked, performers were often recognized during the day. It was good for business to be at their best whenever in public.

Our usual nightclub booking lasted two weeks. Most clubs had two shows a night, six nights a week. To encourage repeat business, the second week shows were changed from the prior week's.

My sister and I became Manhattan Models in 1953. Thus began the most fascinating, fun, adventuresome, and memorable times of our lives.

Manhattan Cocktail Review 1953 Show Photo. L-R: Joann, Pat, Jat Herod, Betty (Bryant) Herod, Allene, and Penni.

Part One

~

American Gypsies

Poster for Amato's Supper Club, Portland, Oregon, November 1953.

Chapter One

January 1, 1955

Now that it's 1955, I guess I should get busy with some resolutions.

Gee whiz! I'm almost eighteen and have been a dancer for almost three years already. I still don't miss school and the kids back in Anacortes because this is more fun. What I like most about dancing in a revue is all the traveling we do. Two weeks here, two weeks there. The Manhattan Cocktail Revue really gets around!

Joining the revue was Allene's idea. Being an older sister, she sort of makes our decisions and I go along. That's okay. She's great at making resolutions too. I think it was her 1952 resolutions that got us into show business in the first place—wanting to be famous, to meet millionaires, to dance with Gene Kelly, to travel, and to drive a car. We've managed to do three out of five, which is neat. (Fame and Gene Kelly could take forever!) Anyway, her 1955 list is bound to include Dick, her latest heavenly hunk of man. After all, he kicked off the new year by sending her a dozen long-stemmed roses from Los Angeles. The bellboy here at the Hermitage Hotel had to hunt all over for a big enough vase.

Some of the nightclubs Jat Herod's Manhattan Cocktail Revue books us into are not so great—kind of smoky and dirty. But others like the Iroquois Gardens here in Louisville are super. Last night for New Year's Eve the crowd at the club was terrific. Not drunk or noisy at all. Since celebrating the new year is a special event of sorts, we had a stripper on the bill with our revue. She was not a regular stripper like the kind who just walks around dropping off her clothes to music. This one had a flock of birds undressing her. It was really something to see! She kept the birds in a cage backstage, and we had to skirt around it to make our entrances and exits between numbers, being careful not to bump it and disturb the birds. She would yell at us if we got too close. I don't blame her. Those birds were very important to the success of her performance. I've always wondered how she trained them.

Today, New Year's Day, business was slow at the club. Allene and I didn't have much to do between shows but sit around and listen to the band, so our boss's daughter, JoAleene Herod, talked us into helping her break in her puppet show. This little girl has been thoroughly fascinated with puppets since she received one last year for her tenth birthday—and had been learning the ukulele before that. I think all six of us in the show are glad the kid switched interests. We got totally tired of hearing her strum the Davis and Mitchell "oldie," "You Are My Sunshine" over and over every day.

Anyway, after clearing a space in the dressing room, we put on our miniature performance for Betty and Jat. A two-cent admission fee bought JoAleene's parents ringside seats plus some day-old Hydrox cookies. The Herods' daughter made the puppets from cardboard she'd colored with crayons and our theater was cut from an Old Crow shipping box. While JoAleene and I did the puppets, Allene worked the stage lights (a flashlight she borrowed from the kitchen help). Our three plays went very well. It helped that Betty and Jat got into the spirit by cheering the hero and hissing the villain. Kind of fun. I think Betty, who grew up on a showboat and has been an entertainer all her life, especially liked seeing her daughter take it upon herself to create this little show: writing plots, dialogue, exits, and entrances.

Had to hang around after work for a band rehearsal since we're changing routines next week. The Herods are putting in the Beach routine to replace the Charleston as an opener. The Beach is more of a production number with costume changes onstage and lots of comedy, thanks to Jat and Betty with their jokes and songs. Also, the Oriental will go in for a closer instead of the Gypsy routine. Didn't get back to the hotel until daybreak.

January 2, 1955

It's Sunday and our day off, so Allene and I went to Calvary Church this morning. The minister and quite a few of the congregation remembered us from last year when the Manhattan Cocktail Revue played Louisville. Didn't expect to be back in Kentucky at this time, but there was a sudden change of plans. We all thought we were going home to the West Coast for the holidays. I should know by now that nothing is certain in show business! Not even the contract we had to work the popular Cave Supper Club in Vancouver, BC.

According to Jat, the Cave's manager couldn't pay Nelson Eddy, who'd just worked the club, his full salary so he gave him an IOU for the balance. Of course, an IOU was fine with a wealthy, famous singer like Nelson Eddy, but somehow the union got wind of the deal. They pasted a sign on the door and shut down the club. And it will stay shut until the manager can cough up what he owes Nelson Eddy. Too bad. The closure has affected a lot of people like the eight-piece band, waiters, bartenders, cooks—all out of work now during the big season.

I guess I should be thankful. At least we're working. But I'd sure like to see Mom and Papa, and I know Allene would too. The Herods tried hard to make Christmas in Louisville as merry as possible for their dancers. They even put up a tree in their hotel room and had the goodies and the presents, but, of course, it wasn't the same.

Stayed in the hotel this afternoon sewing silver beads on a new white costume for the singing act Betty has been working up for Allene and me. There'll be inch-wide snowflakes all over the bodice and solid bead fringe on the leotard. Lots and lots of sewing but should be beautiful when it's finished. While sewing bead after bead, we listened to the radio in our hotel room. It plays three hours for fifty cents. Allene figured out how we can save time if we happen to leave the room before our three hours are up: just pull out the plug. My sister's pretty smart.

Around dinnertime, Betty stopped by our hotel room to inform Allene and me our hair still looks "muddy" on stage under the lights. It needs to be blonder. That means we've got to leave the smelly bleach on our heads longer. Betty went on to say, however, that our new curly bangs look good. We're lucky the home permanent we used on top of our bleached hair gave us a decent curl with no frizz. It was Allene who dreamed up the idea of bangs and a perm. Seems one night while riding in a convertible, her pinned-on curls came loose and almost flew off her head!

January 4, 1955

Had a nice surprise later today. Mr. Gould phoned the Herods to say he was in town. Our best fan from Chicago came to see our shows tonight at the Iroquois Gardens. Between performances, he bought everybody steak dinners and champagne and, for Betty and us dancers, gorgeous purple orchids to wear. Mr. Gould's such a generous person. I think we're like family to him. The seven of us are getting used to his showing up wherever we're booked for an engagement, staying a couple of days, buying dinners and treats, then taking off again. Our friend's probably seen the revue a hundred times, but he always gets a kick out of it anyway, and I wonder sometimes if he used to be an entertainer himself—maybe in vaudeville, playing the two-shows-a-day theater circuit. But he never talks about himself.

Got another surprise during the evening. Colonel Meels in Memphis called the club between shows to talk to Jat about getting the Manhattan Cocktail Revue back to play the Silver Slipper, that elegant Memphis nightclub.

When the revue worked the Silver Slipper a couple of years ago, Snooks Friedman was the owner and bandleader. He was directing the musicians when Allene and I broke in Lerner and Loewe's "They Call the Wind Maria," one of the songs for our singing act. I remember that about the time I took a deep breath and warbled the line "blow my love to me," my zipper blew, letting in cold air! I shivered and shuddered as chilly metal slipped slowly down my back. Did the rest of the act with one hand behind me, clutching my costume together. Got some lively applause at the end, but I don't think it was for my singing.

January 5, 1955

Allene got a letter from Dick telling her how much he would like to see her again. My sister gets so excited when she hears from him. He's a really nice fellow and has pretty, cool blue eyes, but I think Dick's too old for her. Besides that, he's divorced. I guess he's a charmer, though, always laughing and joking, lots of fun to be with. Still, Allene knows very little about him. And she won't ask either, I'll bet. Probably, it's too early to ask, afraid she'll spoil the budding romance. As far as I'm concerned, he's too much on the surface, but Allene wouldn't agree with that. Personally, I prefer Don from Denver who's always sending my sister big boxes of chocolates— which I get to eat.

Today, we had to send off to Mehron's for some new false eyelashes. Mine are coming apart and Allene's are stuck together much of the time. It's a good thing Betty doesn't insist we wear full lashes on stage anymore. They really bothered Allene and me. Mine would hit my eyebrows when I looked up, making it hard to see. With Allene, the lashes irritated her eyes and made them water, causing the floppy things to droop on one end or come off altogether. A bit embarrassing. Now, we use half-lashes and can split one pair of full eyelashes between us. Works great and saves money.

Lucked out with a potential costume catastrophe tonight. During the second show, which had a small audience (thank goodness), my halter top broke while I was twirling around and clanking finger cymbals in the Oriental number. Hard to miss my predicament as the unfastened straps flew out whenever I turned. I danced holding my breath, afraid the top, held only by a hook and a snap across my back, would slowly slip to my waist! Jat stood off to one side of the stage and watched me intently with a worried expression. I suppose my face was turning blue from lack of oxygen. Anyway, I made it through the number.

January 9, 1955

Last night was our closing as well as Peg's birthday. Peg's been with the revue longer than Allene and I have and is a terrific dancer. It's all Allene and I can do to kick as high as she does. For chorus line uniformity, Peg has to actually hold back. I think if she kicked as high as she is able to, she'd probably hit her head with her knee every time. Anyway, we had a party for Peg between shows. The band played "Happy Birthday," and everyone in the club sang while Peg sliced into an enormous ice cream cake. Allene and I split one yummy wedge, while little JoAleene helped herself to three big pieces. (Average for a growing girl!) Penni, Peg's dancing buddy who joined the revue at the same time she did, bought some champagne to sip while Peg opened her gifts. Although our birthday girl had only a skinny piece of cake, I noticed she downed several glasses of champagne. As a result, Peg fairly "glowed" all during the second show, especially in the Oriental number, when she giggled on stage and turned so fast, her hat slid down over one ear! Betty observed Peg's distracting behavior but didn't say anything to her afterward. Birthdays come but once a year.

That wasn't all that happened last night. I had to put in my two bits when I went off after the Beach number by turning and falling down the stairs leading to our dressing room. I clattered all the way to the bottom, losing my beachball and umbrella, snapping the heel right off one of my platforms and, finally, crashing into some serving trays. You'd think I'd been the one drinking champagne! Saw anxious faces looking down from the top of the stairs, but I said I was okay, picked up my props, then hunted around for the heel, which a waiter picked up and handed to me. Good thing it was our last show.

Got up early this morning and checked out of the Hermitage, then waited around for the Herods, who finally arrived about noon in their brown station wagon, pulling the little wardrobe trailer. They'd have been here earlier, but apparently last night, Jat locked his keys in the station wagon. This morning he had to smash the wing window to get the door open. Unfortunately, a policeman saw him breaking the car window with a brick, and Jat then needed to prove the vehicle was his.

Anyway, it seemed to take Jat forever to load all our stuff into the station wagon. Poor guy. Cigarette holder between clenched teeth, our boss pushed and shoved suitcases around. He struggled with bags, coats, luggage, hats, and shoes. Allene and I felt kind of guilty. Living on the road, we've managed to acquire more than the allowed two suitcases apiece. I know that if we ever hit a bump and ran off the highway, passengers in the station wagon would be buried under an avalanche of belongings, costumes, and props! Luckily, the other two dancers in the revue travel separately, so they can take some of the luggage. That helps. Penni drives her own car, a green Plymouth that's been across the country more than once. Peg's usually with her. Since they are pals from dancing school days in Seattle, Penni and Peg pretty much go everywhere together.

Finally, got away from Louisville at about noon after Jat slammed the tailgate shut, headed for the driver's seat, and yelled, "Saddle Up! Let's hit the road." The station wagon started off with a terrific lurch. I banged my head on the window, the Herods' Chihuahua, Cheekaboom, who'd been on Betty's lap, tumbled to the floor, and JoAleene, who'd been on the suitcases in the back, rolled onto the seat between Allene and me. Everyone had a good laugh, which is a nice way to start a long jump.

January 10, 1955

Trip south through Tennessee was good, except for one episode that kind of shook up Jat. He was just cruising along talking about show business, like he often does, and remarking that TV is causing nightclubs to close or to cut back entertainment, when suddenly the car just ahead of us slowed, allowing us to pass. Then, we heard a screaming siren and got pulled over. It was a cop! He'd been going eighty-five miles an hour chasing a speeding car and wanted to know why we were on his tail, also going eighty-five miles an hour. Jat said he thought he was keeping up with traffic. The cop was nice and let us go, but Jat was pretty quiet after that.

Drove into Nashville later and passed the Plantation Club, where we worked two years ago. Met some great people at that time, mostly politicians celebrating something by spending a bunch of money on dinners and drinks. I remembered this club was also where I caught my big toe in the hem of my gypsy skirt coming down some stairs onto the dance floor. To the rousing strains of Jat playing an energetic gypsy melody on his violin, I fell and slid, tambourine and all, right under a ringside table. Stopped myself from smacking into a table leg by grabbing a man's ankle! He pulled up the tablecloth, looked at me, and laughed his head off. I didn't think it was all that funny because I was under a table instead of on the dance floor with the others. But maybe it was. Anyway, we never got booked there again.

Once past the Plantation Club with its memories, we drove into downtown Nashville, after passing a chain gang of men at work on the road. We went to dinner at Cross Keys, a dandy place for a fast meal, since it's a cafeteria. By the time we got back on the highway, it was raining and pretty dark. Off-and-on showers stayed with us all the way to Chattanooga, and, wouldn't you know it, the city was torn up with some big construction project. Had to take a muddy detour through the city. Really surprised me to see some people lived in bare-board houses raised off the ground on bricks and used kerosene lamps instead of electricity. Just like back in the last century.

Around midnight, somewhere in Georgia, the station wagon backfired, jerked forward, then rolled to a stop by the side of the road. Same old thing. Jat had run out of gas. Our boss waits until he's just about on empty before he even starts looking for a station. And it has to be one with cheap gas and a prize for every fill-up. Leaving us locked in the station wagon, Jat got out his fuel can and went walking. Closed my eyes and tried to sleep but couldn't get comfortable. All of a sudden, Betty cried out. There, on the passenger side, was a man in a white suit and big straw hat looking in at us! He tapped on the window, and Betty lowered it about an inch. The man asked her if this was the way to Miami. He said he couldn't remember how long he'd been walking but thought he must be getting close! Betty said, "Yes, yes," motioning him away. He then smiled, tipped his hat, and went whistling down the road at a good pace. Wonder if he made it.

Jat had managed to hitch a ride to and from a gas station, so we weren't delayed by the side of the road more than half an hour. He'd bought enough fuel to get us to one of his cheap gas stations with prizes. Good thing because by then, we all had to go to the restroom.

Fully gassed up and moving again, the station wagon became like a rocking cradle, and I fell asleep listening to Jat compose another one of his hillbilly songs. This one was all about trying not to fall in love with his best friend's sweetheart or something like that. Kind of Hank Williams style, but not so depressing.

I really think our boss is country western at heart, although to hear him play classical and jazz violin, you'd never guess it. It's not just the music he writes but the way he dresses when driving between jobs—jeans, cowboy boots and hat, leather jacket—like he was on his way to a rodeo! Wearing the Western outfit probably gets Jat into the mood for thinking up words and music to create country songs, his special way of staying awake, while driving when everybody else is conked out. Since he's sold a few things to Nashville publishers, I guess he knows what he's doing. Anyway, the soft singing's kind of neat to hear when everything's dark and quiet. Always has me nodding off in no time.

I woke up when I heard Jat and Betty talking about making a breakfast stop. Always ready to eat, JoAleene came to life too and slid down onto the seat with Allene and me to comb her hair and put on her shoes. It was daybreak and we were just entering Atlanta. After eggs and grits at a 24-hour café, we continued south through red dirt fields and big oak tree country until we arrived in Albany, Georgia. By then it was midmorning. Checked into the New Albany Hotel in the center of town. Spotted the old, green Plymouth, so knew that Peg and Penni had arrived ahead of us. Once in our room, Allene and I unpacked and hung up some clothes before letting the whirling overhead fan lull us to sleep.

All too soon our alarm went off. It was two o'clock and time to go to band rehearsal. Drove with the Herods out the old highway to the Paramount Club. The place hasn't changed since we worked it last year—still resembles a big, old, dingy white house built at the edge of a swamp. We went inside to the rehearsal by way of the backdoor, and I noticed a cotton ball dangling from a string nailed dead center. There was one there last year too. Betty says it's some voodoo thing to keep evil spirits out and was put there by the kitchen help. Seems to me, because of the swamp and swarms of insects, it could be a homemade wad of bug repellent.

Rehearsed for three hours with a local band under the direction of Bill Grassick and learned we do three shows nightly, instead of the two we did during our previous engagement. That's because there's a new owner. We actually only have to put on two different shows, since the third one will be a repeat of the first. The bad part about doing a third show is having to hang around the club into the wee small hours, which makes for a long evening. Also, except on weekends, there may only be a handful of people in the audience— often slightly tipsy by the time the final performance rolls around.

Returned to our room at the hotel where Allene and I ate some fruit for dinner since there wasn't time to go out anywhere. We put on our stage makeup, then changed into our black and gold cocktail dresses before pinning one another's hair up into a chignon of curls. This is something new for us. We've been wearing our long hair in a pageboy style. This hairdo is Betty's idea to make us look more sophisticated. Suits me. At least my crowning glory is pulled back out of my face and stays put! The Herods called our room at about 7:30 p.m. to see if we were ready to drive with them back out to the club.

Our opening night went well at the club, and we had good crowds for all three shows. Saw lots of familiar, smiling faces in the audience to make us feel welcome. Boy, all of us were really tired by the time we got out of the club, back to our hotel rooms, and to bed.

The original Manhattan Cocktail Revue in four photos taken by Bloom, in Chicago, Illinois, in 1947 as follows:

Top left: Betty Gaylord, Betty Bryant, Jat Herod, Toni Gaylord
Top right: Jat, Betty G., Betty B., Toni G.
Bottom left: Toni G, Betty B., Jat, Betty G.
Bottom right: Betty G., Betty B., Toni G.

*Allene showing an audience member
how to do Russian kicks at Club 509 in Detroit,
Michigan, in 1954.*

*Pat (L) and Allene (R) doing their
Russian dance routine at Leroy's Club in Honolulu,
Hawaii, May 1954.*

Chapter Two

January 12, 1955

Woke up at noon and went to the post office first thing to pick up mail at General Delivery. Our new eyelashes arrived, plus we got letters from Shorty in Augusta and Joe in Anchorage. The weather is clear and sunny—very pleasant—so Allene and I took a long walk through Albany and found an Episcopal church we can go to this Sunday, then we returned to the hotel.

I like Albany, and I'm glad we're booked here again. It has a quaint and small-town feel with its big, moss-dripping magnolia trees lining the avenues, the easy-going atmosphere along with a sleepy, old southern charm. Kind of neat. Downtown there is a wide, clean-swept-looking main street, but not much else. Reminds me of back home in Anacortes, except here in Albany severe thunderstorms can dump tons of rain and gigantic water beetles on everything. No one seems to mind though.

Had just settled down to sew beads when Betty called with some bad news. Seems the new club owner/manager isn't happy with our routines. I noticed that this guy was eyeballing us pretty good last night. During each of the three shows, he sat ringside with his arms folded, scrutinizing and scowling at every little thing we did, not laughing, not even cracking a smile at anything! Charming. Anyway, had to drop all we were doing this afternoon to go to another rehearsal. Rushed out to the club and did a crash run-through of possible replacement numbers like the Cakewalk, old Gypsy, Oriental, and then the Jungle which none of us remembered. Worked a couple of hours smoothing out dance steps and floor placement, then Betty kept Allene and me after Peg and Penni took off. She wants us to add a new song to our act plus develop a jazz toe routine. Ouch.

My sister was extra pleased and gung ho at the news. The reason we joined the revue in the first place was to get material for a good act while dancing for a living. Since her whole life has been in show business, Betty Herod knows a lot and we're flattered she wants to keep teaching us more and more. Actually, I think she enjoys seeing her ideas developed for performance. That includes songs, dances, musical arrangements, hand gestures, visual comedy, everything. She reminded us today that it's not just a case of memorizing songs and dances for an act; personality and appearance onstage and off are just as important. According to our boss, to be successful in show business, Allene and I must: 1. Look like showgirls on and off stage; 2. Be cheerful all the time; 3. Always be eager and ready to work. Sounds reasonable.

Anyway, this afternoon Betty completed gestures for the song in our act but didn't even get started on the jazz toe routine. That's okay with me. I'm not crazy about doing anything on my toes, because I know it's going to hurt like anything! Of course, Allene loves the challenge. Had another good crowd at the club, except for the third show, where the audience was all on one side of the room, and some of us had to work to empty tables. I find it kind of tempting to goof off when a performance seems more like a rehearsal. However, according to Betty, stage presence must be maintained no matter what, so I behaved myself.

Met a couple of characters, Bob and Dick, who are air force pilots. They were at the club throughout the evening drinking and dancing, so saw all three shows and insisted upon taking Allene and me to breakfast. Went to Stem's, a really good café downtown that's always open. Both guys seemed very nice but very chatty. One is from Cleveland and the other is from Memphis. Naturally, we heard all about those places. They wanted to show us Turner Air Force Base not far from here, but Allene said no, thanks. It was already dawn.

January 14, 1955

Allene received a letter from Dick today and was all aflutter. He's still in Los Angeles clearing up some legal matters so he can chuck California and move to Wyoming. I don't blame him for falling in love with Jackson Hole. He's okay in that respect, but I still think he's too old for my sister.

Wrote a letter to Elaine. Our older sister was not pleased when Allene and I first went into show business. But now she thinks it's neat that we can see so much of the country and that we're in a successful revue. She and her husband, Pete, even drove up to see us in Vancouver, BC when we played the Cave Supper Club last year. She always asks how our act is coming. I told her about our impromptu rehearsal with Betty yesterday. Walked to the library after that for a little exercise and education. Allene thinks it's necessary to keep up with the latest news—plus we need to know more, period. We read articles in magazines like *Life*, *Redbook*, *Time*, and *Ladies' Home Journal*. They're okay, but seem more for people who just live in one place and want challenging things to do or think about. We like *Variety* and *Billboard* too, which at least tell about clubs and shows across the country, but not all libraries offer those magazines.

On the way back to the hotel we saw a place that rents all kinds of bicycles. Both of us then felt like going bike riding, except the weather was too cold. I don't think the Herods would have approved anyway. They'd be afraid we'd fall off and break something, I'll bet. Like the time when the revue was booked in Anchorage in January. Allene and I weren't going to let all that snow and ice go to waste. Being great admirers of Sonja Henie, the ice-skating movie star, my big sister and I bought ice skates and took lessons at an outdoor rink. The Herods knew about it and were nervous, sure that one or both of us would sprain, break, or bruise something. Actually, I did fall and bang my head, but only got dizzy for a while. I could still dance and didn't miss a show. They worry too much.

Wish the revue could go back to Alaska, even though when we were there it was dark and below zero most of the day. But the buildings were really interesting with their wavy floors from all the freezing and thawing, and I liked seeing moose on the outskirts of

Betty (Bryant) Herod, center with cane, and showgirls (L-R) Pat, Joann, Penni, and Allene.

town along with distant snowy mountains everywhere. Allene and I ate in our hotel room a lot, I remember, because it wasn't easy to get out to cafés. We'd buy groceries then use our window as both a freezer and refrigerator. Quite convenient.

Tonight, we were pleased to see Betty's parents, Captain Billy and Josie Bryant, at the Paramount Club. They are visiting from West Virginia and came tonight for our first show of the evening. This week we're doing the Beach routine, where we strip down onstage, behind parasols, from ruffled dresses to sequined bathing suits for some high kicking; the Ladyfinger Revue, our miniature show within a show; the Old Lady Bit, vaudeville comedy with lots of gags; and the Gypsy, with swirling skirts and jingling tambourines. Like Mr. Gould, I guess Betty's folks have seen our show a hundred times but still seem to enjoy the jokes and routines.

Right afterward, JoAleene and I put on the puppet show (now called the Zany Puppets) for her grandparents backstage. Allene helped again by handing us tiny props and doing the spotlight—a flashlight loaned from the bartender this time. Things went very well until I knocked over our cardboard theater with my elbow and had to take a short intermission to pick up the pieces.

The Bryants roared at that mishap, plus our squeaky voices and antics as puppets batting one another around. I know they were tickled their granddaughter is doing these shows and, in her way, carrying out what Captain Billy and Josie began fifty years ago with their showboat, presenting melodramas and variety shows in waterfront towns along the Ohio River until 1943.

There was a good crowd at the club for our first two shows but hardly anyone was around for the third. With so few people in the audience, Jat did the performance all by himself, playing requests on the violin, everything from classics to some hillbilly and Western tunes (his favorites) thrown in. Between the cowboy numbers, our boss told a bunch of gags with the band vamping clippety-clop, clippety-clop rhythms in the background like a trotting horse. One joke was about a little boy being late for school because he had to take the bull down to the cow so they could get a calf next spring. The teacher said angrily, "Well, couldn't your father have done that?" And the little boy answered, "Yeh, but Mom thought the bull ought to." Ha! Then, he'd talk about how much he enjoyed horseback riding and add, "I was tall in the saddle till my blister broke." That always gets good laughs.

Tonight, because the Bryants are riding with the Herods, Allene and I got a ride back to the hotel with Peg and Penni in the Plymouth. Beyond doing shows and being in the same dressing room, we don't see much of the other two dancers. Nice to touch base once in a while. After taking off our makeup, Allene and I went to their room where the four of us sat around eating raisins and talking about nothing in particular.

Then, while pulling off her false eyelashes, Penni told us that JoAleene had BIG news. She said that yesterday the Herods' daughter whispered in her ear that her father, Jat, has a chance to work the theater circuit in England and Scotland! Nothing is set yet, but they expect to hear from the London agent soon. Peg, smearing cold cream all over her face, said she wouldn't be surprised if the Herods do leave the country. After all, she added, they must be tired of the same old clubs, same old towns, same old routines. Then, she grabbed a handful of tissue and started crying about missing her boyfriend, Red. She went on and on about all the fun the two of them had when the revue was booked at Leroy's Club in Honolulu. That was where she met him between shows one night. He was stationed at Pearl Harbor and, that night, had taken her driving along the beach and up to Diamond Head in a convertible. She then blew her nose and said she'd never forget his big grin and wonderful laugh when he'd suddenly throw his arm around her. Well, I didn't say anything but, personally, I think it was Hawaii, not Red. Living in a balmy, romantic place for four months does things to people.

After we went back to our room, I told Allene I thought the whole idea of the Herods leaving is scary. If they go overseas for several months or even a year, what will the four of us dancers, the Manhattan Models, do? All we know is performing in their revue, and we depend on them to handle bookings, rehearsals, agents, club managers, you name it. My sister reminded me that JoAleene could be wrong. Although the Herods' daughter is a good "spy" for us, her info often turns out to be a bum steer, she said, like the time we were "for sure" booked in Winnemucca, Nevada, and it fell through.

Didn't get to bed until about the time the birds were chirping. Woke up later with a stomachache. Too many raisins.

January 18, 1955

Received letters from Mom, Tom, Joe in Omaha, Ray, Brian, and Francis. Mom reports she is spending most of the money we send her on renovating the old house Papa bought that sits on a hill overlooking Anacortes. The view is great, Mom says. She can see Guemes and Cypress Islands, Cap Sante, Mt. Baker, and, on a clear day, the Alexander Selkirk range near Vancouver, BC. First thing she wants, then, is a huge picture window across the living room. Because it's a little house, Papa is thinking of enclosing the front porch and making it a dining room.

After reading our mail, Allene and I took a walk into downtown Albany. Shopped for something new to wear and found cute cotton dresses at Lois Annelle's. They are exactly alike—just what we need since we're billed as twins—in black and white with lace trim. I think we'll be able to wear them to clubs, but we'll certainly check with

Betty first because she's pretty strict about how her dancers look both on and off stage. Bought fruit, cereal, and milk at the Colonial Market, then returned to the hotel.Back in our room, we put fifty cents in the rent-a-radio and listened to Doris Day and Pérez Prado while sewing the costumes for our new dance number. This routine is another specialty spot for us and will have lots of turns and kicks. Betty designed the outfits, of course, and they're going to be pretty wild! Allene and I will wear black and white polka-dot bikinis with three-foot-wide melon-colored bustles attached to our rear ends. Topping that off, we'll balance tall, tube-shaped hats trimmed with black boa feathers on our heads.

Tonight, out at the Paramount Club, during the Old Lady Bit in the second show, Betty did six encores. (The audience went crazy over her eccentric dancing!) The bit starts when Jat sings "Sweet Adeline" and Betty comes onstage in a dumpy, dowdy costume to flirt and joke with him. They get a lot of laughs and go on for about ten minutes with Betty never cracking a smile. Finally, Jat asks if she can do anything and Betty says, "I sing." Jat replies, "What?" Betty answers, "Songs." Then, she adds, "I cry when I sing." Jat asks why and she replies, "I can't sing." Jat, exasperated, says, "Well, can you dance?" Betty responds, "Uh-huh", then takes off across the floor, hopping and jumping around with crazy-looking dance steps, even before her music begins. She's a riot.

To close the second show, Jat pulled out the Gypsy and replaced it with the Audience Dance Participation, because the club manager wanted to see a "livelier" number. Anyway, Penni, Peg, and Allene got three guys up to do a ballet, boogie, and Cossack dance respectively.

Allene demonstrated a sequence of steps for the ballet contestant and coached him as he tried to do the dance. The poor fellow looked totally lost and uncoordinated. He couldn't even stand on one leg for an arabesque or a kick!

The biggest challenge was for the Cossack dance contestant. Peg demonstrated the routine which includes Russian hocks, where a person squats down, folds their arms on their chest, and kicks straight out front. Tonight, the dancer, like most others who've gone before, fell on his keister and got a laugh.

The boogie dancer, Penni's contestant, was the best. Wiggling from head to toe, he bounced around doing the Shorty George boogie step, which is difficult for some guys, but this fellow was obviously having a ball. He gave me a kiss on the cheek (nice little surprise) when I came onstage and handed him a bottle of champagne for winning first place.

Then, Jat got carried away joking with the boogie dancer winner, telling him he looked so dignified and reserved until he got up on the stage and shook everything but the "kitchen sink." And because this guy had a receding hairline, like Jat's, our boss did a bunch of jokes about going bald and wearing toupees. All that would have been okay, except I had a fly crawling up my leg, and couldn't do anything about it but stand there through it all and smile! Darn pest. Better on my leg than on my nose, I guess.

After the show, our boogie expert, whose name is Cal, poured each of us a glass of the champagne he'd won, so Peg, Penni, Allene, and I sat at his table awhile, then took turns twirling around the dance floor with him. Cal's a marine from Tampa and sure is a good dancer. Cute too.

Had to hang around the club after it closed for a band rehearsal. Guess the club owner isn't happy with any of our numbers because Betty says he wants a whole new show for tomorrow night! The Herods are replacing the Beach, Gypsy, and Oriental with the Mambo, Cakewalk, and Football. Good thing they carry a ton of music and loads of wardrobe in the trailer. Didn't get home until daylight.

January 20, 1955

Allene received letters from Eggie in Grand Rapids, Jim in St. Louis, and Dick in Los Angeles. Jim loves Allene and wants her to come to St. Louis, and Dick says he will fly over to Chicago if she can meet him there. Allene won't do either, but I know she's having fun thinking about it. Eggie's trying to get us booked at the Elks in Grand Rapids in May for some big party. Nice idea, but who knows where we'll be by May. Peg and Penni want to go to Miami for a week when we leave here. Since our next job isn't until February 5 in Des Moines, Iowa, they plan to enjoy the beaches and clubs around Miami before heading north to cold weather. Allene and I don't particularly want to go to Florida but really have no choice. The Herods are going up to Point Pleasant, West Virginia, for a week to stay with Betty's parents, so we'll be without transportation. Oh well, that's the way it goes. What the heck! We've never been to Florida before. We might even like it.

Had good audiences for the first two shows tonight and met some colorful characters in between. First, we chatted with Johnny and Joe, who are in the Nassau dress business and work out of Pensacola. They had on such dazzling shirts. I'd love to see the kind of dresses they sell. Also, met Bob and Bert, twins from San Francisco, on their way to Key West for some fishing. Talked with Mike, brother of Carl, the former Paramount Club bartender. Allene and I miss Carl. He was so friendly and loved to crack jokes as he mixed drinks. Anyway, according to Mike, Carl got married and went to live in Atlanta, which is where he grew up.

Something unusual and exciting happened at the club during the third show. During the part where Jat plays audience requests on his violin, somebody back at the bar yelled out, loud and clear, "Play 'The Great Speckled Bird!'" Jat ignored the demand and took other requests. The guy yelled out again, even louder, "Play 'The Great Speckled Bird!'" Jat yelled back, "I'm sorry, but I've never even heard of it!" *That* got a laugh—and started a fight! In the dressing room, we could hear people getting smacked around, barstools going over with lots of yelling, swearing, and glasses breaking. As if trying to drown out the racket, Jat launched into a popular Western song on his violin as fast as he could! Peeked out of the dressing room in time to see the bartender—with extra help from waiters and customers—shove the fighters out the front door and lock it! Things quieted down after that, of course, but Jat couldn't continue because of all the chaos, so he introduced the Manhattan Models ahead of schedule for the Football routine, and we had to scramble to get onstage—ready or not!

Cal, our dancing Marine, sat ringside the whole evening, clapping like mad for all our numbers, and apparently enjoying the added excitement of the bar brawl. Anyway, he took Allene and me to breakfast at Stem's after work. He looked so cute wearing a charcoal-grey suit with a pink shirt and flowered tie. (Wow!) I think he likes my sister. But then, she's more fascinating than I am.

January 22, 1955

I got up at noon and, first thing, went over to Peg's room to help her bleach her hair. Allene and I can do one another's hair, but Peg doesn't have anyone. Penni, who rooms with Peg, uses a red tint on her hair so is totally unfamiliar with hair lightening. Anyway, all Peg did was sit and talk about Red, describing in lengthy detail his hair, his eyes, his extra-wide shoulders, etc. I felt trapped having to listen about how wonderful this guy is while I painted smelly Roux and peroxide foam on her roots with a toothbrush. Was glad to finish and go back to my room.

Packed suitcases after that, since we'll be leaving here soon, and had to sit on a couple of them to get them closed! For sure, we'd better send a box of stuff home. Then, Allene and I messed around singing and dancing a bit, especially working on our new dance routine. Betty gave us some African drum music to listen to which might help us "absorb" the routine's rhythms. Also, since we'll be in Miami, she suggested we shop around for palmetto fans to use as props.

Had a really jolly bunch at the club tonight. I met a fellow named Freddy who turned out to be a mambo expert. Got to dance with him between shows, and it was all I could do to keep up! Fun trying though. Freddy gyrated from head to toe and did spins all over the place, really attracting attention. Betty wasn't a bit pleased. She felt Freddy was an exhibitionist and inclined to make a dance partner look mediocre. (Ouch!) Well, I guess it's just like trying to keep up with someone who loves to jitterbug. Betty says, unless you've danced with them before, you're apt to either get injured or look like you have two left feet. That's why she won't allow Manhattan Models to jitterbug—or even mambo now, because of Freddy.

Had to laugh. During the Football routine tonight, Penni accidentally dropped the football and had to chase it down, pick it up, and throw it—too late for any of us to catch. We had to go on with the play, ball or no ball. So the football sailed past us and out into the audience where some lovely lady in a strapless cocktail dress jumped up and caught it! She stopped the show cold and got a well-deserved hand. Jat shouted out, "Lady, you can play on my team anytime!" He meant it too.

Between the second and third shows, JoAleene and I put on our Zany Puppets for the club owners of the Paramount because they had taken an interest in this little girl who was always backstage with her dolls and puppets. Well, she *is* good and always well-behaved. Not many people see her though. It's funny how JoAleene dresses up to come to work every night, just like the rest of us, with her long hair pulled back and a little mink stole over her outfit, looking like a miniature showgirl. That's how it is when you're raised in show business.

Anyway, the Herods' daughter and I broke in a scene from the opera *Hansel and Gretel* with Allene singing "When at Night I Go to Sleep." Turned out great and we got terrific applause (probably because of Allene's singing), so we went ahead and did the other four puppet routines in our repertoire. The club owners applauded like mad again. I told JoAleene afterward that we had enough material now to do an act. For a minute she really thought I was serious!

Met Jim and Drew, cute guys with crewcuts from Turner Air Force Base. They'd won some bucks on a barracks bet so were on a spending spree and took Allene, Peg, Penni, and me to Stem's for breakfast after work. Peg was a little tipsy and talked endlessly about Red. (What else?) Earlier today a gorgeous Hawaiian orchid lei arrived from him as a reminder of their first date. Charming.

Packed when we got back to the hotel and went to bed around dawn.

The Ladyfinger Revue (photo by Bloom), Chicago 1954.

Old Lady Comedy Routine with Betty and Jat, Hilltop Casino,
East Dubuque, Illinois, 1955.

Chapter Three

January 23, 1955

The Herods left today, bound for West Virginia. Since we have a week off, they are taking some of their belongings for the Bryants to store while they are in Great Britain. Found out our "spy," JoAleene, had good info after all. Jat opens in Glasgow on March 14 doing a single act, playing his violin, and telling jokes. This will be quite a departure for him. Since 1949 when he and Betty joined forces with a song and dance act called The Gaylord Sisters to form the Manhattan Cocktail Revue, he's been part of his own complete show. After adding two more dancers, the Herods worked hard cranking out the special material, routines, and costumes for their little revue. And it has all paid off in several years of solid bookings.

Now I wonder if Jat's sick of the responsibility of trying to keep a six-person act booked. Or perhaps our boss wants to take a crack at being a star! The Herods have not said much; just that they're "trying something new." The three of them sail on the French Line's *Île de France* next month. Betty seems to think the four Manhattan Models will do all right on their own for a while. Sure hope so.

Soon after the Herods drove out of Albany, it started snowing. Looked out our hotel window and watched young boys dancing around trying to catch the falling flakes. Probably hadn't seen the white stuff before! Packed up the Plymouth and finally left Albany in the late afternoon bound for Miami with Penni and Peg. By the time we got on the highway going south, the lovely snow had turned to rain, which drizzled down on us the rest of the day.

I fell asleep halfway through Florida and missed the Everglades. It was dark anyway. Woke up about dawn when we were twenty miles or so from Miami. What a sight! Long white beaches, rolling swells on a green ocean, and a pale blue sky that just kept going.

Arrived in Miami Beach at breakfast time, and, first off, drove along the oceanfront gawking at the string of huge, fantastic hotels, with their tropical gardens and sparkling pools. Can't afford that! Penni knew of a place from a previous trip, so we went there and checked in. Not bad at all. Although a small establishment, the hotel, called Ocean Haven, has a big patio and pool. It's right on the beach with surf sounds within earshot—if we leave our window open.

Before we even unpacked, Allene and I hurried out, bought swimsuits, changed, and, all excited, rushed for the beach. Ho! Ho! Ho! Despite sunny skies, a cold wind whipped in off the ocean giving us goosebumps. Allene sat in the sand with a shirt on, content to just look at the sea. But not me. I figured the water, at least, must be warm, so I went galloping into the rolling swells, got smacked by a chilly wave, and immediately came running back out again. Disappointed, Allene and I headed back to the hotel, and, on the way, met Leo and Trent, who said they were card dealers from Las Vegas. I believe it. They were tan as tumbleweeds and couldn't have acquired that here! Anyway, these guys, shivering in their plaid swim trunks, said they were on vacation from smoky gambling rooms and desert heat. Leo asked Allene and me if we'd like to play catch since we couldn't enjoy the ocean, so we formed a square and threw a tennis ball around for a while. Then, Trent asked if we'd like to go to dinner someplace tonight. Allene lied and said we had plans. Pretty soon the wind got stronger and ruined our game of catch, so we said adios. Hope we'll see them again.

Back at the hotel, Allene and I changed into our colorful Hawaiian pedal pusher outfits and were sitting around with nothing to do when Penni came to tell us that Tom, a friend of hers, had just arrived in his own plane. And he wanted to take the four of us out to dinner—right away! (I think my sister must be psychic about evening plans.) Went to a great place called The Embers and had a luscious dinner—steak and lobster, pineapple pilaf, asparagus spears, and some sensational fruit sherbet creation for dessert. Allene and I felt like beach bums, though, in our pedal pushers. Looking around, we couldn't help but notice that other diners were really dressed up. Guys in snazzy silk suits and gals in fabulous gowns and jewels. Welcome to Miami Beach!

January 29, 1955

We've been in Miami four days now. Last night Allene and I walked over to the Pickin' Chicken for dinner. Had to laugh. About the time our dinners arrived, a really good-looking fellow sat down at the table across from us and smiled at Allene. Being a pleasant person, she smiled back. (My sister has a great smile.) He promptly invited himself over and sat next to her. A bit pushy, I thought, yet kind of charming and from New York. Funny too. He said he'd come to Miami Beach to find a wealthy woman needing an escort and willing to finance his singing career! I choked on a French fry considering that one.

Our "friend" paid no attention to me and ordered himself some chicken. I glanced at my sister. Allene sat stiff and staring like someone had just dropped a bug down her back. Did he think she was rich? Would we end up with his dinner tab? In the end, our talkative friend just wanted to tell someone of his plans for snaring a rich "pigeon" and, I think, feel out if we could help. That's a crack-up.

This morning we went sunbathing, but it was cold (as usual), and we gave up (as usual). Seems to me, January is *the* season in Florida. Right now, I could use some fuzzy socks and long johns.

At about noon Allene decided to look up our cousin Bruce. A relative we've never met, but we know he lives in Miami Beach. After finding his phone number in the directory, Allene called him. As luck would have it, Aunt Jean, his mother (another relative we've never met), was in town for a visit, so the two came an hour later, picked us up, and off we went to the Seven Seas for lunch. Very nice restaurant! Had a shock right off the bat though. Aunt Jean knew today is my eighteenth birthday, and she wasted no time telling me she thought I should go back home and finish high school! She thought three years of moving around, singing, and dancing in a show was enough. If we still want to travel, she went on, do it with books. She reminded us that we were the first ones in the family who'd gone into show business.

We talked of other things, of course. Still, Aunt Jean's so-very-freely-given advice shook me up. Rationalizing my feelings, I decided that Aunt Jean, being a retired librarian, would say something like that. Although we hardly know her, she seems to know us.

It's funny about the birthday business. Since Allene and I are now twins, we don't celebrate my birthday anymore. I celebrate with Allene. The twins' gimmick has been fine since we joined the revue. I remember Betty Herod took one look at the two of us dressed alike, and decided since she couldn't tell us apart, we should henceforth be twins. It sounded better in our billing. Suits me.

Back at the Ocean Haven, Murray, someone Peg and Penni met last night, called and said he wanted to take the four of us out for dinner, then to see the Latin Quarter floor show. Allene told Penni we'd love to go since we only have a couple of days left in Miami and haven't seen any of the famous clubs and shows. Later, Peg said Murray called again informing her that he had some buddies coming over and that dinner and drinks before the Latin Quarter would be in his room. So Allene told Peg to forget it. With that, the whole plan collapsed. Feeling very disappointed, I suggested we take in a Donald O'Connor movie being shown tonight by the pool. Better than nothing.

The four of us sat in the hotel lobby watching the Eddie Cantor Show on TV when Penni got a phone call. It was her pilot pal Tom, who, with his friend Abe, wanted to take everybody (again!) out to dinner! Went to Wolfies this time because Abe loves their ham and cheese on rye and strawberry cheesecake. Slid into a roomy booth where we enjoyed some laughs and sandwiches. For dessert, each

Pat and Allene with Aunt Jean (center) in Miami, Florida, January 1953.

of us ordered a different kind of cheesecake then divvied up and swapped pieces. The waiters watching us had a good laugh. Strange dinner with lots of food and nothing fancy, but a nice change.

The six of us squeezed into a cab and went to the Beachcomber Club after that. Saw the Ritz Brothers performing their nutty comedy, mostly visual stuff like they did in the movies years ago. Then, it was Louis Armstrong with singer Thelma Middleton raising the roof with their music. A really fine show. Spotted Milton Berle in the audience chomping on a cigar.

Went from the Beachcomber to the Vagabond Club and caught the last show. On the bill were the Three Dunhills, terrific male dancers, doing precision tap dancing, shoulder to shoulder much of the time. The Vagabonds were the headliners, of course, and they did a great act, but about halfway through, one of them suddenly walked off the stage and didn't return! The others kept glancing at the wings as they continued playing, so this obviously was not part of the act. Found out later that the guy went out to the parking lot and shot himself. Not fatally. Just enough to scare everyone.

Then, as we were getting ready to leave, a couple who had seen us perform at the Hilltop Casino in East Dubuque, Illinois, came over to our table to say hello. Gosh, we get around.

January 31, 1955

Penni packed the Plymouth last night, so we were able to leave Miami bright and early this morning: 6:30 a.m.! Didn't stop for breakfast until we'd gone north about 150 miles. Lots of daylight and sunshine during this trip, so Florida looked a lot better today than it did a week ago.

Stopped at Cypress Gardens to take in the water show and admire the pink flamingos. After our week off, Allene and I didn't feel we could pay the full price of admission. But we did feel daring. Quickly, putting our hair in braids and removing our makeup, we got in for under twelve years old (fifty cents apiece). Peg and Penni walked on ahead like they didn't know us. Oh well. Then, because we were such cute "kids," dressed alike and all, Allene and I were given a big sack of free oranges. Feasted on them the entire way to Silver Springs, where we took the glass-bottom boat trip and had dinner.

Peg drove from Silver Springs to give Penni a break. Rolled into Albany, Georgia around midnight and got dropped off at Banks' Pecan Courts, located outside of town in an orchard. Allene and I plus the Herods stayed there two years ago, the first time we worked at the Paramount Club, and prefer it to any hotel downtown. Trouble is, it's inconvenient without a car. Mrs. Banks was surprised and happy to see "the twins" again, and, despite the hour, invited us in for ham sandwiches and milk. As we sat at her kitchen table eating, we told her about being in Florida and how different it was compared to Georgia. Allene remarked she liked Georgia better because it truly represents the South, whereas Florida is kind of a composite, with people from all sorts of other places. I prefer Georgia too, but I'm not sure why.

Got settled in our motel room and, before going to sleep, Allene commented that it's too bad we won't be staying more than a day. I had to agree. Banks' Pecan Courts is like living in the country with a caring family, not like a regular motel at all.

February 2, 1955

The Banks gave Allene and me a large bag of pecans from their orchard to take on our trip north. Our next booking isn't until February 5 in Des Moines, so Penni plans to have a pleasant drive, stopping to see friends we know on the way. I like that.

Didn't leave Albany right off. After picking us up in the morning, Penni took the Plymouth to have the engine checked, wheels aligned, and all. Because we had nothing else to do, Allene and I strolled over to the library. Read some magazines and newspapers to find out what President Eisenhower's been doing besides playing golf. After about two hours, we walked back to the garage and still had to wait and wait for the Plymouth to get finished. Finally left Albany and started north in the late afternoon. The four of us felt pretty jolly to finally be on our way. It had been a long day of just sitting around. Once underway, Penni decided our first stop would be Anderson, Indiana, where Joann, a former dancer with the revue, is living.

Unfortunately, we didn't get very far. Somewhere near Atlanta we heard *POW! POW!* Pieces of rubber came flying out from the bottom of the car. Penni immediately slowed to a snail's pace, and we wobbled into the nearest gas station. Had to wait until a new tire could be put on.

Back on the highway, hopes for making up lost time collapsed when it suddenly became dark and stormy, with flashes of lightning and plenty of rumbling, all of which turned into one terrific thunderstorm. Heavy, heavy rain made the windshield wipers useless, and the turbulent wind whipped us broadside. Looking in any direction there was a watery blur, so Penni crept along while the three of us watched the edge of the road (as best we could) to be sure she kept the car on the pavement. The storm passed quickly enough. Lucky for us!

Kept driving steadily north and got as far as London, Kentucky, before the Plymouth died altogether sometime after midnight. Luckily, we were inside the city limits instead of miles out in the dingles! Spotted a nearby garage and waited, doing our best to stay warm while keeping an eye on the place, until the bright lights came on and the big door went up. Penni cornered a mechanic right off, but, unfortunately, he had a backlog of jobs to finish. We got something to eat in a dingy café down the street, then doodled around with nothing to do and nowhere to go. Super. It was noon before the mechanic could diagnose what ailed the Plymouth. He replaced some blown valves and we set off again.

Midafternoon, back on the road, we settled down and even joked about the lousy journey so far. Enjoyed a pleasant drive through Lexington and Frankfort—until the Plymouth struck again. *POW! POW!* Another tire exploded, shaking us up but good. This time we were about ten miles from the Indiana border.

Lucky for us, the blowout happened right in front of a farmhouse, where someone inside must have heard the bang. Just as Penni came to a screeching halt by the side of the road, a man came rushing from the place. Being a nice person, he changed the tire for Penni, right then and there. Our Good Samaritan mentioned he repaired cars for a living, so we drove to his shop just down the highway, where he fixed the blown tire, then checked all the others. Penni paid him and thanked him profusely before we drove off once again.

Managed to get the rest of the way to Anderson, Indiana, our destination for this leg of the trip, without another blowout or breakdown. It was late at night when Penni pulled into the familiar driveway next to Joann's house. Frazzled, but thankful to have finally arrived, we just sat in that bad luck, never-to-be-trusted-again green vehicle.

None of us had seen Joann since she quit the revue about a year ago. We were sorry to lose her because she was such a good-natured, agreeable person to work with. I always thought she was a terrific tap dancer too—light on her feet, fast-moving, and getting the most sound out of a wooden floor. With enough space, she could dazzle you with Ann Miller-type turns!

Anyway, Joann was very happy to see the four of us and swiftly assembled a bunch of ham sandwiches, which we gobbled down.

Then, after such a horrible trip, we just conked out on the couches in her living room.

February 3, 1955

Sat around all morning talking about some of the places we'd worked together with the Manhattan Cocktail Revue. Joann mentioned the time we played Detroit and did continuous shows at the 509 Club, a place where the audience didn't applaud—they banged on the tables with little wooden hammers instead! There were characters like Fuzzy, a blond midget wrestler who loved to jitterbug, and the old English colonel who came over from Windsor, Ontario on Sundays for dinner and to waltz with Betty. Also, there was Max, the bookie, and Tiny, the tout, along with various sober hoods and drunken sea captains. In its way, the 509 was remarkable, I guess. One night the Detroit Lions arrived in a group expressly to see our football number, where we toss the pigskin around, block, kick, run, and all that. They loved it! The guys banged the tables so hard that the little wooden hammers shattered and went flying. Best of all, though, the team autographed our football.

As for performers, strippers were always on the bill with us at the 509. Joann remembered one who was so friendly and funny, always joking. She was a tiny thing with bright red curly hair, big brown eyes, and a great smile. We really enjoyed working with her. Then, one night, being slightly inebriated, she danced too close to the edge of the stage while unfastening her bra and fell right over—a three-foot drop. The band played chaser music as Jerry, the bouncer, carried her off. I don't think she broke anything, but we never saw her again.The Herods wanted to spiffy up the revue, so we broke in a big (for us) production number at the 509 called The Merry Widow based on Lehár's operetta. All of us Manhattan Models concentrated on being elegant and sophisticated in our long, black velvet "Gay Nineties" gowns and huge feathered hats, strolling around Jat as he played "Vilia" on the violin. Boy, did we look classy! Then, stripping down to corsets, we launched into a fast cancan with jump splits for the big finish.

We worked hard in Detroit with continuous shows seven nights a week for six weeks straight and rehearsing practically every day. However, we managed to find time to see some great shows while we were in town, usually matinee performances. These included a ballet, an opera, and a comedy. We did manage to catch The Four Freshmen's evening performance at a nightclub when we arrived in town a day before our opening. That was special because the four of us were great fans of the quartet and had been ever since Penni let us listen to their recordings on her little 45-rpm record player. We even had a chance to chat with them during their break. Really special!

Peg brought up the time we did shows in Anchorage and Seward. I remember Alaska as being a mixture of dogsled races, bear hunters, jet pilots, and navy bean soup served from a bucket on the back of a Seward café's stove. Then, there was the night Betty hurried us from the Anchorage nightclub just as the manager, thoroughly zonked, pulled out a pistol, and started shooting from the back of the bar! Alaska was still the Wild, Wild West.

I was impressed the night a prospector came in bragging about his claim, poured gold nuggets from his sack onto the bar, and ordered drinks for everyone.

Allene said the best thing she saw in Anchorage were the sled dog races down the main street of town during the Frontier Days celebration. Penni chimed in with, "Yeh, but how about the Indians' Blanket Toss! That was really something. Those fellows were being thrown at least twenty feet in the air!" I had to admit that was sensational.

After lunch with Joann and more chitchat about clubs we'd played and cities we'd seen, the four of us reluctantly said goodbye to our friend and pulled out of Anderson, bound for Chicago and a night out. Unfortunately, the Plymouth altered our plans once again. Didn't drive very far before the speedometer stopped working. Not knowing her speed, Penni had to slow down, so we lost time and didn't arrive at the Croydon Hotel in Chicago until nine o'clock, which left us no time to relax or get cleaned up. Found Mr. Gould and the three Herods patiently waiting in the lobby as we hurried to check in. Rushed to our rooms and changed clothes as fast as we could. Meanwhile, Mr. Gould got two cabs, which took us over to the Chez Paree for a late dinner, orchids, champagne, and the show.

As usual, we had a ringside table. The last time Mr. Gould took the seven of us to the Chez Paree we saw Jimmy Durante on stage doing his vaudeville act where he demolishes his piano for the big finish. An added treat was seeing his old vaudeville pal, Sophie Tucker, in the audience.

This time, we enjoyed Lena Horne's show. She looked gorgeous, just like in her movies, standing like some goddess in a tight satin gown as she sang, surrounded by a chorus of handsome male dancers in tuxedos. Sensational!

Jat, Betty, Candy, Peggy, Pat, and JoAleene with crew ready to go fishing in Hawaii.

Babalu routine at LeRoy's Club, Honolulu, Hawaii. Candy in the center, with Pat (L) and Allene (R) in black wigs. June 1954.

Chapter Four

February 5, 1955

Left Chicago yesterday after Mr. Gould bought breakfast and lunch, then took us to the early show at the Chicago Theater to see Billy Eckstine, a favorite of ours with his ruffly shirts and nice deep voice.

Hit the road for Des Moines, Iowa, following a fond farewell to Mr. Gould, our generous friend, who paid for everything, including our hotel bills. The Herods left ahead of us. Didn't have much chance to talk to them, but they seemed to have had a good time in Point Pleasant with the Bryants. Well, I'm sure it was a nice change for them, especially JoAleene, to stay in a house and live in a town where everyone knows one another. Penni said that JoAleene even met some kids her own age.

The four of us drove first to Dubuque, Iowa, intending to stop to see Roger, an old boyfriend of Penni's, on our way through. However, we ran into snow as we neared town. It looked like it meant business, so Penni decided we'd better get rooms and stay the night in a motel, rather than just dropping by Roger's in a storm. There was snow everywhere when we went out to visit him and his mom in the morning. Over a great ham-and-eggs breakfast, we chatted about the threat of more freezing weather, the arrival of exotic plants at the family's flower shop, and the new band at the Hilltop, a club we played last fall, located across the river in East Dubuque. Got back on the road again around midmorning.

Finally reached Des Moines at noon today and checked into the Elliot Hotel downtown. This is the first time we've been to this city, and, so far, Des Moines looks flat and cold and windy. (Makes me wish we were back in the South!) Anyway, we are here for the week to do a big auto show starring Julius LaRosa, a popular singer from New York, originally promoted by Arthur Godfrey on television. The singer made some records, and did a couple of TV shows, but mostly sings on the radio, I think. Neat voice, really handsome too. Unpacked a few things before we drove over to the large, new convention center, where we are to perform at the Des Moines Auto Show. With construction materials lying all around, it is obviously an unfinished project, but complete enough to allow people to use it. Our dressing room is something—an enormous concrete box of a room with wires dangling from sockets in the walls and electrical outlets poking out of the floor. I managed, first off, to trip over one and cut my ankle. Plus, there's *no heat*! Super.

Met the Herods at the center for band rehearsal. Surprise! Surprise! The public had been invited! Instead of an empty auditorium, we looked out at several hundred people with cameras and autograph books sitting as near as they could to the stage. They hadn't come to see us, of course, but to get an up-close, unobstructed view of Julius LaRosa in the flesh.

Unfortunately, the main attraction didn't even show up. Another person rehearsed LaRosa's music for him. The disappointed crowd waited and waited for hours before slowly making for the exits.

Rehearsal ran late. It seems we are part of a very big show and, of course, all the acts must do a run-through with the band. We hung around hoping for a chance to practice our routines on the great big, raised platform that was our stage, but no dice. Time ran out. Betty dismissed the four of us so we could get something to eat before showtime. Hurried to Bishop's for roast beef sandwiches, then rushed to the hotel to put on our makeup and get back over to the convention center. The Herods never had a chance to leave the place. It was six o'clock before Jat rehearsed our music with the musicians, so he had to zip through everything because the show was at seven o'clock.

Our first performance started right on time and went without a hitch. Grabbed my first glimpse of our star, Julius LaRosa, smoking a cigarette backstage while waiting to go on. He looked at me, smiled faintly, and said he didn't feel well. He might have said more but didn't get the chance.

Bright lights . . . Drumroll . . . Cymbal crash! "And now, ladies and gentlemen, the star of our show" . . . and Julius was on! He quickly took one last drag, stubbed out the cigarette, then strolled casually into a waiting spotlight. The singing star's music commenced, but it was impossible to hear! The crowd had exploded into a din of screaming, clapping, and stomping. Graciously accepting the noisy adoration, Julius bowed, then stepped up to the microphone. The minute he opened his mouth, a great hush fell over the audience. It was as though someone flipped a switch. Julius had them in his pocket from the start. I've never seen such an adoring audience—like he was some sort of god.

Julius sang, looking and sounding fantastic. After the performance, fans swarmed onto the stage. They blockaded the dressing rooms, keeping all of us busy signing autographs and posing for pictures. Kind of neat.

February 7, 1955

Allene left first thing this morning to locate a grocery store, while I picked up our mail at the post office's General Delivery. Received a letter from Mom saying that Papa went out and bought a '53 powder-blue Buick with white-sidewall tires and three holes on each side of the hood. The little "portholes" indicate the size of the engine, she wrote. Two holes mean less horsepower while four means more, so Papa got something in between. He sure likes his cars. I can just see him waxing the finish and polishing the chrome. This car sounds big and fast, just what they need for their Sunday drives to Sunset Beach! (I'm joking.)

JoAleene came by the room later to show Allene and me the newspaper with its headlines and long write-up advertising the Des Moines Auto Show. Naturally, there was a big picture of Julius LaRosa. The four Manhattan Models (that's us!) were shown on another page, perched atop the backseat of a convertible in our Charleston costumes, waving at the crowd of admirers pushing autograph books at us. Hey, this is the life!

Did a matinee today and the gigantic auditorium was jam-packed with at least a couple thousand people. They were a terrific audience, clapping and whistling, and we enjoyed every minute of performing for them. The closing act was Julius LaRosa. Again, I watched him as he stood backstage, looking pale and miserable, smoking and waiting for his introduction. Poor guy. But even though he isn't feeling a bit better, he did a bang-up show again today, with his fans screaming for more. He says it's his stomach bothering him and told Allene earlier he may have to go back to New York. I hope not.

My sister and I really like Julius. I'm not sure Betty does, though. She says there's nothing wrong with LaRosa's stomach—it's his head. Our star is one of those people, she says, who believes New York City is the world and anything beyond Manhattan Island is the "boonies," which he wants no part of. If that's true, I guess he's spoiled and opinionated, which I find hard to believe. I think Julius is quite pleasant and reasonable. He's so soft-spoken and really handsome, with dimples and dark curly hair—just like his pictures—and I can't believe he'd just up and leave because Des Moines isn't New York. He sure looked sick to me.

February 8, 1955

This morning JoAleene pounded on our door, waking us up. She told us her father got a phone call, bright and early, informing him that Julius is gone! Our ailing star left on a morning flight for New York. I guess things are in an uproar as a result. Promoters of the auto show are angry with Julius for leaving, sick or not, and the car dealers have started a lawsuit against him, JoAleene said. Her father is already on his way to the convention center to find out what happens next.

Allene moped around after that news. She enjoyed watching Julius from backstage when he sang and is quite disappointed he deserted the show when so many people depended upon him. I think she has a crush on him. (*That's* my sister.)

Rehearsed today in our hotel room because it's too cold to go down to the auditorium. Betty worked with us to finish our new specialty number before she sails for England on the French Line's *Liberté* in a couple of weeks. I don't know how she comes up with the steps she does. There'll be exaggerated hip-swinging while we're doing the Latin moves, plus there are backbends and kick turns, all at a fast pace. I just hope we can manage it all in our black heels, hauling three-foot-wide bustles.

Had to laugh when Betty mentioned that both of us have made an art out of "faking" routines. She says Allene and I will do a step all wrong, but, because we're always together, it looks fine, and like we know what we're doing! She went on to say that Allene has a tendency to squint when she smiles, and if she wants to look her best—which of course my sister wants that more than anything— she'd better practice smiling in front of a mirror, making sure her eyes stay open.

As for me, Betty commented that I get shrill (and annoying, I presume) when excited and should concentrate on lowering the tone of my voice at every opportunity. Well, maybe one of these days the Halliday Twins will be perfect!

Late this afternoon, The Four Step Brothers arrived to replace Julius as headliners of the show. These guys are outstanding tap dancers and do a terrific act, but it isn't very long. So, a circus-type balancing act has also been added to the bill. We certainly have a variety show now! It's great these entertainers can fill in on such short notice. But the Manhattan Cocktail Revue can do more too. In fact, we could probably do the whole show, if necessary. But, for now, Jat's putting in our Football routine and the Ladyfinger Revue to add more time.

Betty's Ladyfinger Revue is always a big hit. I think of it as a kind of tiny revue within our show, having its own unique little suitcase-size stage with curtains and all. Betty made the dolls out of cardboard and buckram attached to cotton gloves with two fingers cut out of each glove for the doll's legs (which are the "lady fingers") poking through for the miniature dancers. These miniature showgirls dance or parade around in colorful costumes.

Betty's specialty is her "world's smallest tap dancer," where, with metal thimbles on her fingers, she dances her doll across a piece of glass, producing a sharp rhythmic tapping sound.

Had a huge crowd again—several thousand people, I would guess—for the one performance this evening, and then we got a nice surprise. Auto show sponsors were so pleased with everyone's efforts that they catered a big buffet dinner for all the entertainers. Tables full of goodies were set up near the stage after the show. It was a beautiful spread with all kinds of luscious food on giant platters. The whole crew really appreciated the treat.

February 9, 1955

Stuck my head out the window this morning and got smacked in the face by blowing slivers of ice. (Just what we need!) Living in Des Moines, Allene and I have developed dry, chapped skin, so we didn't dare go outside the hotel today even to pick up the mail! I can tell now; this will not go down as one of our favorite bookings.

A blonde singer arrived from Chicago for tonight's show. Her name is Ginny Scott. She uses a lot of specially written material in her act, not the usual popular songs. Her facial expressions as she acts out the lyrics are quite good. She's really cute.

We have enjoyed working with The Four Step Brothers. Unfortunately, this is their last night. Because of a previous booking, they could only fill in for two performances. Darn! I could stand backstage and watch them forever. I've never seen such smooth dancing. Especially the trenches and wings, single and double. At the end of their act tonight they really cut loose, challenging each other with fantastic tap-dancing improvisations and comedy. The thinnest of the four leaped onto the piano (which shook up the poor piano player!) and off again, landing in the splits. Then, as a group, they jumped over and under one another before sliding into splits. Pretty strenuous stuff. The crowd, of course, screamed for more!

February 10, 1955

Stayed in the hotel room all day again, keeping warm and staying well-creamed with body lotion to combat the dry, cracking skin situation. Allene wrote letters to Don in Denver, Bob in Detroit, Jim in St. Louis, Ray in Alaska, and, of course, Dick. I sewed silver beads in snowflake patterns on our new white costumes for the singing act. It's kind of tiresome but faster than doing the solid bead fringe, which seems to take forever and ever.

Before going downstairs to the coffee shop for dinner, Allene and I practiced our new number in the hotel room, shaking and clapping our hands instead of rattling tambourines, which, without a doubt, would have caused complaints up and down the hall. The black and white polka-dot costumes for the routine are coming along fine and are so cute. We plan to add some black bangles to the melon-colored bustles for some sparkle. Other than that, and the black boa trim, the costume is mostly straight sewing and easy to do. NO sequins or beads. Nice change!

On the show with us tonight was Dagmar, the busty blonde TV star, and her All-American Boys. This act replaces The Four Step Brothers, who had replaced Julius LaRosa. Dagmar is very friendly and quite beautiful. The All-American Boys are shorter than she is, but then, Dagmar is statuesque, to say the least. (Something like Anita Ekberg, but more so). She doesn't do much of an act, but I suppose she doesn't need to. I think people just pay to see her in real life. Dagmar has a darling white poodle named Shakespeare that is always with her.

Had fun signing autographs again after tonight's show, mostly for kids. Some wanted to know where Julius was. (Good question!) We were delayed about half an hour seeing to our fans. Ha!

Peg, Penni, Allene, and I finally got out of the convention center and to the parking lot. Bad News! The poor old Plymouth was frozen solid. Penni tried starting the car, and it didn't even click. The Herods had already left, so we thought we were stuck, really stuck, in an empty parking lot on a cold night. As luck would have it, one of the car dealers, also late leaving, came to our rescue and gave us a lift to the Elliot Hotel.

February 14, 1955

We closed Des Moines two nights ago and said goodbye to everybody at the convention center who did so much to make the week's performances a success, despite Mr. LaRosa's departure. Mostly I mean the musicians. With all the different acts coming and going, our band had a very busy week with extra rehearsals, plus playing the shows—and did a fine job.

Allene and I checked out of the Elliot Hotel around noon yesterday, then sat in the lobby writing letters while waiting for the Plymouth to get thawed out. (It had frozen up again during the night.) Left for Omaha, Nebraska, at midday for a fairly short trip. Enjoyed snowy scenery all the way, mostly fields next to the highway, looking so white and sparkling in the afternoon sun. Too bad it's so cold.

We arrived in Omaha, and, first thing, before even getting settled, rushed over to the big Omaha Auto Show. The four of us wanted to see The Mills Brothers, who were the headliners. Managed to catch the tail end of their act and heard them do Hoagy Carmichael's "Up a Lazy River," which is an audience favorite. And ours too!

After four months, it's nice to be back in Omaha for a return engagement. We're staying at the Rome Hotel again. Allene and I went downtown this morning for breakfast at Jack n' Jill's and weighed ourselves on their scale. Allene is 117 and I'm 116. This is different. Usually I weigh more!

Picked up our mail from General Delivery. Allene received valentines from Jim, Dick, Don, Cal, Ray, Francis, and Steve. They all still love her. Don sent chocolates, but the box got squashed, so they don't look good enough to eat. And that's just as well because while getting dressed for our opening night show at Offutt Air Force Base, Allene discovered she's too fat to wear her blue silk sarong from Honolulu. Horrors! I got into my matching sarong okay, but we both struggled endlessly with the zipper on hers and had to give up. With a feeling of defeat, we put on black dresses instead. Not so good. Allene will want to go on a diet now. That means I'll have to stop eating too.

Had a nice surprise this evening. Saw our friends, performers Phil Ford and Mimi Hines, out at the air base. They looked wonderful, just the same as when Allene and I met them in Seattle during our chorus line days at the Showbox in '52. I remember that Phil always encouraged us to work up an act and get out of the chorus—something we're still trying to do! We'd see him and Mimi down at the Showbox rehearsing routines for the new double act they were creating, or at the Cornelius Hotel, where most of the show people (including us) stayed while in Seattle. Anyway, they played Offutt Air Base last week with their music and comedy act, then stayed over in Omaha to see our opening.

Phil Ford and the Herods have known one another for years. According to our "spy," her folks are going to work with Phil and Mimi on their act, revising some of the things they do, and offering suggestions on how to get more laughs. I know Betty feels Mimi should do comedy because she's perky and funny, especially when making faces or chirpy sounds. Like Phil, Mimi goes for a gag in her solo act anytime she can find one.

The band at the air force base is the same as last year and excellent. Joe Herman, the fabulous bongo player, is still stationed at Offutt, so, like before, Jat wants him to do a couple of solos as part of the show. Joe's so good, our boss said, he used to back up Peggy Lee, doing bongos for her special singing arrangements.

Allene was upset all evening about getting fat. She kept looking in the full-length dressing room mirror, turning this way and that, holding her breath, pinching her sides, and poking her tummy. Yes, her costumes are snug, but that's really not so bad. First, we are doing the Mambo this week, a shake-it-don't-break-it number. The little two-piece white costumes we wear are deliberately too tight. Betty has each of us squished into and overflowing those cute little scraps of satin, bangles, and ruffle-laden material because nobody wants to see scrawny dancers.

Second, we're doing the Hoedown, where we're in gingham formfitting dresses and straw hats. Allene had to hold in her sides while I inched up the zipper for her. I thought she would cry! Penni was a help, though, telling Allene how "busty" she looked now that she's heavier. Except for Peg, who's really stacked, the Manhattan Models routinely pad out their costumes with falsies, socks, or something. Bigger is better, topside anyway.

Had to laugh at Jat tonight during the Hoedown. He really got into the spirit of a country square dance by putting on his cowboy hat, stomping one foot, and fiddling away, fast and furious. Then, the audience started clapping in time and whooping it up. Turned out to be lots of fun for everyone.

Jat threw in another joke tonight. Went like this: An analyst brought two boys into his office—one, a pessimist, the other, an optimist. The analyst put the pessimist in a room full of toys and after an hour's time went in to check on him. The kid hadn't touched a thing. The analyst asked, "Little boy, why haven't you played with these toys?" The little guy answered, "You're just trying to trick me. You're going to take them all away." The analyst then put the optimist in a room full of manure. After an hour he went in to find the boy having a wonderful time digging, tunneling, laughing, and throwing the manure in the air. The analyst said, "This is amazing! Little boy, why are you having so much fun? It's only a pile of manure." The boy replied, "Well, with all this manure, I figure there's got to be a pony under there somewhere!"

After work, JoAleene came back to the hotel room with Allene and me, instead of going out to eat with Phil, Mimi, and her folks. She said she wasn't hungry. The three of us then stayed up until dawn playing Scrabble and a geography game. We talked about JoAleene's upcoming trip to Scotland and England, but the kid didn't seem very interested. Or very happy. I would be excited about visiting places like London, Edinburgh, Cardiff, Glasgow, and maybe even Paris, and I said so. Even when I showed JoAleene where those cities were on the game's geography board, she wasn't impressed. To lift the kid's spirits, Allene gave the Herods' daughter the box of smashed chocolates. That, at least, made JoAleene smile.

February 16, 1955

Betty knocked at our door about noon, wanting to pin the black boas on our new costumes and get us started with a Mexican routine. Took Allene and me by surprise! The Herods usually sleep well into the afternoon. I think Betty got up early because she feels time is running out (which, of course, it is) before the big trip and she needs to finish her projects. In any case, we weren't even up. I told our boss when I opened the door that neither of us felt well, and that's why we slept in. So, she went away.

The truth of the matter is that my sister, who everyone knows is a consistent early bird, wanted to sleep longer today because she was dreaming about Dick. I couldn't tell Betty that. Can't let her know Allene is daffy over Dick, because if my sister's in love, really in love, Betty Herod will fire her. According to Betty, a girl in love is not concentrating on her performance. "You love the stage," she says, "or you love a man. It can't be shared." Or something like that. And every Manhattan Model knows how Betty feels. Peg's careful not to talk about Red in front of the Herods. Still, I can't believe Betty hasn't noticed a change in Peg with her bouts of depression and drinking. I don't think Allene is in love, but we can't afford to let any of the Herods, including JoAleene, even suspect it. I believe it's a game with my sister. She's enjoying the attention of her guys and maybe wondering what it might be like to be married to this or that one, especially Dick, but she's not really serious.

Anyway, just before walking back down the hall, Betty mentioned the latest news: Julius LaRosa is being sued for breach of contract for leaving the auto show abruptly. Uh-oh!

Went to the post office to check General Delivery. Got letters from Francis, Ray, Tom, Cal, Paul, and Dick. Allene became dreamy-eyed reading Dick's letter. Guess he still wants to meet her somewhere in the Midwest, if she can fit him into the show schedule. Romantic, but not very convenient. In a happy daze, my sister responded immediately, and we hurried out to mail the perfumed letter informing him she still cared, while not encouraging him to come.

Stopped at Jack n' Jill's on the way back and weighed ourselves again. Allene is 116 and I'm 115. Still too much even though we're eating less! Allene says *we* have to lose five more pounds, so *we* will only eat one meal today—cottage cheese, dates, and a banana. Humph.

Came back to the hotel and began repairing an old rhumba costume for Betty. Some of the sequins have tarnished and need replacing, plus the hooks and eyes are dangling loose. I don't know which routine it's for (probably something she did years ago), but

Betty will pay us $10 to do the sewing. Allene and I plan to take turns. Right off, I anchored down a few hooks and eyes.

Afterward, because Allene didn't feel like doing her sewing shift, we practiced our singing act in front of the mirror. Haven't had a chance to perform this act lately, so really needed to go over hand motions to those songs. Then, we ran through our entire act using a broom commandeered from the maid as our microphone. Stuffing shoes around the broom head, I propped the thing up in our waste basket. That way we can't forget this all-important stage necessity I call our skinny partner. The Herods are always after us to sing directly into the microphone, but Allene and I are so busy watching the audience and remembering our hand gestures, we almost forget it's there. We've made a point of practicing singing with cotton in our ears too. For some reason, plugging our ears helps us stay together and on key. (Jat Herod's idea!)

Did an early club date tonight in downtown Omaha at the Hotel Fontenelle for a hardware convention, working with singer, Tommy Leonetti, and an act called Frasarri and Reynolds. The show was in a basement banquet room, but our dressing room was on the second floor. Had to take the freight elevator back and forth—a bit inconvenient and a challenging race to make costume changes. We almost missed the intro to the Gypsy when the four of us got a ride up to the sixth floor before the elevator headed down to the basement! Besides the awkward dressing room arrangement, we had a little scare onstage during the show. Moving around barefoot in our hula routine, I noticed broken glass on one side of the dance floor and signaled my discovery to the others by motioning toward the jagged pieces. No one got cut feet, but the routine was spoiled because instead of smiling at the audience, we were all watching the floor. Oh well.

After the club date at the Hotel Fontenelle, we changed clothes on the double and piled into The Herods' station wagon, rushing to make our regular show at Offutt. Jat gunned the accelerator, and we tore out of the hotel parking lot and onto the highway, heading for the air base. Unfortunately, we were going too fast. Almost immediately, the station wagon got pulled over, and there was nothing to do but agonize over the time it took the officer to write out the ticket for speeding. In frustration, Jat chewed angrily on his cigarette holder, almost biting it in half!

All this made the show at Offutt late. We hurried to the dressing room only to find it as cold as an igloo, because the heater had conked out. Frantic with frustration, Betty led the way by scooping up costumes and hauling them to the ladies' restroom. We were able to do all our show changes there, although it was a bit crowded with women coming and going. At least it was warm.

Jat put in another new joke tonight: A little boy asks his father where people come from and the father answered, "We all come from dust." Then, the little boy wanted to know where people go when they die. The father responded, "We go back to dust." The boy thought a minute then said, "Well, I think you'd better check under my bed. There's someone either coming or going!" Got a good laugh.

Because JoAleene came by our room after the show with her games again, we were up until about three in the morning playing Scrabble. Peg and Penni dropped in this time, so all of us had fun eating raisins, talking, and straining our brains for words, cities, and countries. I have the distinct feeling JoAleene will miss her "big sisters" when she leaves in a few weeks.

As yet, the Manhattan Models have no bookings lined up and nowhere to go once the Herods are gone. Scary.

Betty, JoAleene, Jat, and Cheekaboom on vacation, 1954.

Lady with the Shaker routine (music written by Jat) at Leroy's Club. Betty in foreground, with Pat, Peggy, Candy, and Allene behind (L-R), Honolulu, Hawaii, June, 1954.

Chapter Five

February 22, 1955

Today is Betty Herod's birthday, so Allene and I got up early and went shopping. Found a pretty, black, hand-beaded evening bag at Herzberg's. We hope she'll like it. It's sure to match several of her cocktail dresses.

Weighed ourselves at Jack n' Jill's one last time. Good news. We're both 114! Back at the Rome Hotel we packed our bags, checked out of the room, then sat in the lobby for a couple of hours reading magazines and waiting, waiting, waiting. The Herods are always late.

It was dark when they finally showed up in their station wagon. Fortunately, we were only going to Lincoln, Nebraska, about sixty miles from Omaha. Once on the highway, we played Twenty Questions at JoAleene's insistence. Betty complained right off that Allene and I always know what the other is thinking, be it animal, vegetable, or mineral, so guessing our topics is easy for us, but puts others at a disadvantage. Getting the correct answer is hard for outsiders like herself, she just *had* to say. Well, I can understand the problem, but I sure don't know how to fix it. I should think the same thing applies to married couples in regard to knowing what's in the other's mind, but I didn't say anything.

After that, Allene started singing the way she does, going from one song to another like it's a set routine, but I know it isn't. She's memorized a lot of songs, that's all. I remember when we were kids on the backyard swing, we'd play a game, singing back and forth. First her, then me, then her, then me, starting off a new song. And if I wasn't quick enough with mine, she launched into another song and won because she knew more songs. That's how we were discovered by a neighbor, who asked Mom if we could sing at the USO for the 1944 Christmas celebration. Mom was delighted. We weren't nervous at all when the big day arrived, and we marched on stage and sang, unaccompanied, every song we knew from the Rodgers and Hammerstein hit musical *Oklahoma!* We won over the audience of soldiers, sailors, marines, and others. Some encouraged Mom to get dance lessons for us so we could get into show business. That's what she did, and we began entertaining for various celebrations and activities in our hometown regularly.

We have sing-alongs in the car too. Usually Allene starts things off by singing songs from Broadway shows and tunes by Cole Porter. The Herods and I join in. We can go through about fifty songs. Sometimes it is Betty who, out of a clear blue sky, begins singing Civil War songs she remembers from her showboat days. Those are something to hear! Stories of soldiers and their sweethearts, marching through Georgia, memories of Mom's cooking, hills of home, the old farm left behind, and stuff like that. Best of all is when Jat starts trilling, "On the Trail of the Lonesome Pine" and, as always, Cheekaboom joins in, howling away. This seems to be the little dog's favorite song—or the only one she knows. It's surefire if anyone sings that song, she'll make it a duet! All singing stops after that. Cheeka's a hard act to follow.

Not finding a cheap gas station in time, Jat rolled to a stop a few miles from Lincoln. He got out his fuel can, as usual, and started walking up the highway, but didn't have far to go. We could see a Shell sign just up ahead. In no time, we were back in business and arrived at the Italian Village, a small but charming nightspot we worked last year. Phil Ford and Mimi Hines were appearing there, and we wanted to see their new act. We checked into the motel next to the club.

Phil and Mimi opened with a fast song, then some jokes. Phil is mostly the straight man now and Mimi's the comic delivering the punch lines. And, boy, did she get the laughs! Then, Phil played the clarinet and did a whole army routine, like Jat, mostly about basic training: living in barracks, eating in a mess hall, group physical exams, and all. Then, Phil, at the piano, accompanied Mimi, who's a terrific singer. They did a fine show, seeming to really enjoy themselves, and got great applause. Not everyone watched Phil and Mimi, though. I noticed the Italian Village has installed a television set over the bar off the main room, and some people just stayed in there watching sports instead of seeing the show. Seems crazy to be watching television while live entertainment is being presented onstage.

Other than that, the Italian Village is still a neat little club that provides delicious food, reasonably priced drinks, and two shows a night. But what's lacking (and always has been) is a decent dressing room for the acts. When we played there, our choice for changing was either the club's restroom or the motel next door. That wouldn't be a problem for Phil and Mimi, because they don't change costumes during their performance. But for the Manhattan Cocktail Revue, with all our routines, a nearby dressing room is not just appreciated. It's vital.

I remember when we were booked at the Italian Village a year ago, Tony, the club owner, had an eight-foot by four-foot raised, curtained platform set up next to the stage for fast changes. We entered and exited via aluminum stairs like trailers and trucks use. The whole flimsy arrangement jiggled when anyone moved within the tiny space. Plus, it was dark inside. (Had to use flashlights to see what we were doing!) Because there was nowhere to hang anything, costumes lay in open wardrobe cases which took up most of the floor space. Pretty bad setup, but we managed fine—for the first few days.

On about the fourth night of our engagement, I stepped backward to let Betty pass, and over the edge I went, falling through the curtain and clattering down the aluminum stairs with nothing on but mesh show hose! I crawled quickly up, then half a dozen arms yanked me back in. Although I'd like to believe only a few waiters saw me, I'll never know for sure. I heard all kinds of laughter and applause, and because Jat was onstage telling jokes at the time, it's hard to say which one of us generated the audience response.

Betty's birthday party was between shows tonight, with Phil

and Mimi providing cake and champagne, while Tony and his brother Ned sent flowers to the table. I think Betty liked her gifts: a robe from Jat and JoAleene, a traveling alarm clock from Peg and Penni, and our black beaded evening bag. Allene and I went off our diet to enjoy great roast beef dinners followed by birthday cake, an Italian creation with several layers of pudding-type filling topped by frosting and nuts, about a thousand calories a bite!

Stayed to see Phil and Mimi's second show, which was funnier than the first, then went back to our motel room with JoAleene tagging along, toting her Monopoly game. Played until midnight. I had Boardwalk and Park Place and Allene bought up the railroads and utilities, while JoAleene made out holding the cheap properties, which she loaded up with houses. Not bad maneuvering for a little girl.

February 23, 1955

Allene and I got up at noon and had a breakfast of dates, cottage cheese, and fruit—stuff we bought at the Central Market in Omaha, so had to finish or toss. The Herods weren't awake yet, so we took a long, brisk walk down the highway. My sister wanted to get some fresh air and exercise since we'll be sitting in the station wagon all day again. She says walking's good for our back muscles and puts "roses" in our cheeks. The weather was so clear and cold, our eyes watered and we had to keep moving right along or freeze. We wandered in and out of a group of side-by-side shops, getting warm if nothing else. Bought postcards and paperbacks (*Learning Spanish*, *Bob Hope's Life*, and *History of England*) for half price.

Saw the Herods back at the motel and found out they had just called Chicago to see if the Manhattan Models have a booking yet. So far, nothing. And the Herods leave for Europe in a matter of days. That's really scary!

Said goodbye to Phil and Mimi, who will be at the Italian Village for another week. Left Lincoln just after lunch and began driving north when Jat suddenly yelled that he couldn't steer straight. We all thought it was because of ice on the road, but turned out to be a tire—going, going, gone flat. Pulled off the road and sat there until, luckily, two fellows in a truck came to our rescue, jacking the station wagon up and changing the tire for us. If Jat had to do the job, we'd still be freezing next to the road. Our grateful boss gave each of them $5 and they were happy.

Arrived at Sioux City, Iowa, in the late afternoon and found the place to be snowier, colder, and windier than either Omaha or Lincoln. The Herods drove by the post office so we could pick up our mail, then we checked into the Jackson Hotel right downtown. Got settled before reading the mail. Within the pile of letters, Allene found one from Jim saying he was coming to visit her—soon! Not in Sioux City, but wherever she goes from here. How romantic.

As I recall, Allene met Jim when he was temporarily stationed for the US Navy in Alaska, and he came with some of his buddies to see our show at the Last Chance Saloon in Anchorage. Jim's home base was Pearl Harbor, so when the revue got booked into Leroy's in Honolulu, he found Allene, and they dated a lot. By the end of our four-month contract, Jim wanted to marry my sister. Guess he still does. Jim's very nice, but Allene is not ready to give up her career for anyone.

Did one show tonight for the Sioux City Auto Show. Like Des Moines, the place teemed with people who were attracted by all the shiny new cars and wanted to be entertained. I'm beginning to think auto shows are a big thing for Midwesterners as a way to break up the bleak, chilly winters! The Sioux City auditorium is not nearly as large as the one in Des Moines, but there are lots of acts—another big show—so we do not have to do much time.

The Manhattan Models opened the show this evening with our Charleston number. While Jat sang, the four of us danced out one by one, then did some really simple kicks and walk-around steps before striking poses. Unfortunately, when Betty came onstage, she caught her high heel on the rutted, well-worn stage surface and stumbled forward. Almost fell. (The audience let out a gasp!) Too bad a dancer can't depend on a floor to be danceable. After all, we need to be smiling and looking at the audience, not watching our every step.

Since I had nothing to do until our Gypsy number finale, I watched the other performers from the wings. Saw the Angels, a balancing act that reminded me of the time I performed with the Anacortes Girls' Tumbling Team at a senior prom. Since we were so wobbly, I can appreciate the strength and coordination it takes to lift others and hold them for a moment. The Angels were followed by The Diplomats, a singing quartet of three guys and a gal, sharp looking with good harmony and plenty of bounce, something like Rosemary Clooney and the Hi-Lo's. Then, it was Roger Ray, a very funny comedian who tells jokes while leaning over a marimba, which he finally did play. Jack Pyle, the emcee, came on after that and did magic tricks with jokes and amusing stories in between. When he finished, he introduced Jat Herod and his violin. I knew my boss would do about fifteen minutes, so I had plenty of time, once he came onstage, to change into my gypsy costume for the closing routine.

Jat isn't doing his usual joke routines because the show is long, but he threw in this one for a breather: "You people out there think all of us show folks are rich, don't you? I'm standing here in a $400 tux, $150 shirt, $200 shoes, $50 cuff links, and $60 tie. But I'll let you in on something. Underneath it all—RAGGEDY UNDERWEAR!"

February 26, 1955

Woke up to snow flurries being whipped around by a gusty wind, so Allene and I stayed in our hotel room. Couldn't rehearse—not enough space at all—so, using our new book, Allene worked on Spanish all morning, and, reading aloud, really sounded like she knew what she was doing, especially rolling her Rs. Besides decent harmony singing, our goal is to have reasonably accurate pronunciation doing Spanish songs for a South-of-the-Border medley we'll put into the act one of these days. Thoroughly in the mood, we practiced a couple of the Spanish songs for the heck of it. The words flow easily and sound so pretty, but I'm not sure what they mean.

Did a matinee today. As to be expected, there were lots of kids in the audience, so a balloon sculptor was on hand busily creating colorful critters, complete with ears and tails.

It was so funny to look across the crowd and see balloon animals bouncing around off the walls and people's heads. Found out after the show that Mr. Gould was in that audience ducking balloons. Our Chicago fan called the Herods earlier and told them he'd be arriving in Sioux City to take us all out to dinner, but first, he wanted to look at the new cars on display.

When the afternoon performance finished, Allene and I got a cab back to the hotel and stuffed clothes hurriedly into suitcases for our next trip. Have to be ready to leave and go SOMEWHERE tomorrow.

JoAleene stopped by and was all aflutter about her big upcoming trip. Guess the excitement of this brand-new experience has finally hit her. First, the three of them will drive to her grandparents' home in West Virginia, she said, where they'll leave the station wagon. From there, they'll travel by bus to New York and board the ocean liner to sail across the Atlantic. The voyage will take a whole week, and then they'll be in England, where they'll see old castles and lots of shows. Like a restless whirlwind that has to be on its way, JoAleene was out the door again. In silence, Allene and I ate our preshow snack of Wheaties, bananas, and milk, then took a cab back over to the auditorium.

Did our final show in Sioux City this evening, and the crowd was terrific. Several hundred people cheering, clapping, and shouting for more make a person feel pretty good. Wish we could stay another day. Said goodbye to the other acts, most of whom will be returning to Chicago for their next bookings. Too bad we couldn't mention where we were going next.

After the performance, Mr. Gould took all of us out for steak dinners. It was a kind of going-away party for the Herods. Following dinner, Peg, Penni, Allene, and I gave the Herods a portable radio with a leather case we'd gone together to buy as a parting gift. They were really surprised and pleased.

Then, Betty tapped her coffee cup several times with a spoon and stood up like she was going to give a speech. Looking around, she said she would miss us, but it was important that they expand their horizons. Change is inevitable, change is good. People should make the most of the opportunities that come their way (and so on). In conclusion, she announced that the Manhattan Models were forthwith launched on their own with their first booking at the Pines Supper Club in Hot Springs, Arkansas, for two weeks with options— beginning the day after tomorrow! Penni will be in charge, Betty said, as far as managing the line, taking care of any bookings or problems, and the person who will pay the bills that come for them. She advised us to support one another and be cooperative at all times. Then, for sure, things will go well, and everything will be fine.

It was hard to say goodbye to the Herods. After all, Allene and I have been with them for three years, playing clubs, going back and forth across the country several times, plus up to Alaska and over to Hawaii for long engagements. We've seen and done so much; it's been like a paid vacation. Right now, I can't imagine doing shows and traveling without this family.

I said *bon voyage* as we left the restaurant, wondering when I'd see the Herods again. Back at the hotel, Penni picked up Cheekaboom, along with her red turtle-necked sweater, leash, and the fuzzy tiger the dog cuddles up to when she sleeps, because the Herods' pet is not going with them. It would have been too hard to take the little Chihuahua overseas since she would have to spend six months in quarantine in England, so she is ours to look after. I know Cheeka will not be any trouble. She can stay in the hotel or motel rooms with us, sleeping on a bed, as she always does, and eating leftovers—usually steak—just like she did with the Herods. Although it was pretty late, Penni packed up the old Plymouth so we'd be ready to leave first thing in the morning.

February 27, 1955

Managed to get a couple of hours sleep before paying our hotel bills and rolling out of Sioux City at daybreak, while everything was still frozen and eerily quiet. It was a pretty straight shot to Omaha, where we stopped for breakfast at a 24-hour café on the north side of the city. Should have gone someplace we know, like Bishop's. I ordered poached eggs, but the cook didn't know how to do that, so I ended up with fried eggs. Not the same. I'm too picky, I guess.

Continued south into Missouri. where there was nothing very interesting to look at in any direction—all pretty desolate and flat. I fell asleep out of sheer boredom. Woke up when Penni announced she was stopping for lunch in Neosho, near the Arkansas border. Deciding it looked halfway decent, she pulled up to a little café with lace curtains and painted window boxes. We all ordered hamburgers that turned out to be too greasy for Allene and me, so the two of us left the place and took Cheeka for a walk. Found a grocery store and bought fruit to eat for lunch and the rest of the trip. It felt great to get out and move around after being in the car for so long, plus the cold air woke me up.

Allene feels that Peg and Penni aren't as adept as the Herods at finding good restaurants on the road. There may be a certain knack to it, or it could have to do with knowing the territory. Looking for cafés with a parking lot full of trucks is good, but not exactly surefire either. Of course, our bosses are familiar with more places because they've traveled all over the country for many years. However, Peg and Penni are driving and can stop where and when they want to. That's only fair.

Crossed into Arkansas and drove through the Ozarks, a scenic area of rolling hills and thick forests we'd been looking forward to seeing. Ha! Ran right into heavy, grey mist and didn't see much beyond the roadside, other than a few treetops poking through. Very disappointing. Driving in and out of fog banks proved scary with repeated slowing down or speeding up on the twisty highway. Terrific. When it got dark, Penni stopped for dinner at a café near Fort Smith. She and Peg went inside while Allene and I stayed in the Plymouth and ate our fruit. Took Cheeka out for some exercise and to smell the smells, but didn't go far because it was too dark. By this time, the trip had worn all of us down. We continued driving in and out of fog through the night, with Penni and Peg taking turns at the wheel. Dismal. There was nothing to talk about. Not much fun and kind of nerve-wracking when you can't see two feet in front of the car!

Finally arrived in Hot Springs by early morning. It had taken us around twenty-five hours to travel the seven hundred miles from Sioux City! Must be a record of some kind. Checked into the Green Gables Motel in town so we could get a few hours' sleep before having to make the early afternoon rehearsal at the Pines Supper Club.

At least we're here.

*Manhattan Models in Cakewalk costumes at Paramount
Club in Hot Springs, Arkansas, 1955, (L-R) Allene,
Penni, Peggy and Pat.*

Part Two

~

The Manhattan
Models Go It Alone

Pat and Jat on stage, 1955.

Chapter 6

February 28, 1955

Up at noon, had something to eat at a nearby café, and got directions from the waitress. Found the Pines Supper Club about one mile out on the Little Rock Highway north of Hot Springs. Seems a bit isolated, with trees and bushes everywhere, and a rather classy country club across the road. Met the owner of the Pines, Mr. MacDonald, who was just opening the club for cleaning. He said there are cabins right next door we can rent. It didn't take us long to decide it would be a good idea for us to live there together to save time and money, so we got one with two bedrooms and a kitchen. The rent's only $25 a week for the four of us. Began moving stuff into our new home right away, but didn't have a chance to unpack before it was time for band rehearsal. Nice and convenient to be next door to the club!

At two o'clock we went over to check out where we'll be performing for the next two weeks, put the wardrobe cases in the dressing room, and just look around. Was surprised to find a good-sized casino, with roulette tables, blackjack, and slot machines off the main room. Kind of different. The only other place we've worked with gambling (that I know of) is Jackson Hole. Lots of poker playing there in the back room.

After the band arrived, we had fun running through numbers on the big, raised dance floor, checking our positions while Penni rehearsed our music, setting tempos and all. Very pleasant musicians (four of them), but the pianist is an elderly man who can't read music! He explained to us that he was not really a piano man, but a trumpet player who lost his lip. Or something like that. Anyway, the clarinetist saved the day by standing next to the pianist and playing the melody for him.

The four of us noticed a good-looking white-haired man, wearing glasses and puffing on a stogie as he watched us rehearse. It was Mr. Stanger, the club manager, friendly, smiling, and quite handsome. Met him afterward along with Mrs. Stanger, a pretty platinum blonde, who strolled into the club carrying a little white poodle. The pooch and the manager's wife wore matching pink bows in their hair and identical pink rhinestone necklaces. Really cute.

Got back to the cabin and found we must be faster seeing to Cheekaboom's needs. Since she never goes outside, the dog is accustomed to using newspapers spread out for her under the bathroom sink. One of us should have remembered that before going to rehearsal. Returned to find a mess in the proper location under the sink. Newspapers or no newspapers, Cheeka had to go and couldn't wait!

Later, the four of us went grocery shopping at Kroger in town to stock our shelves. It's so great to have a stove, refrigerator, dishes, pots and pans, dish towels, eating utensils, and all. We've divvied up the refrigerator and cabinet space so Peg and Penni can have certain shelves while Allene and I have others. Haven't figured out how to split up stove use yet.

We all love the cabin and think it's wonderful—a little old—but still wonderful. Except water comes out of the taps smelling like dirty gym socks and tasting rusty. Also, the toilet seems temperamental, meaning it may or may not flush when you push down the handle. Then too, at least one spider has taken up residence behind the refrigerator. But it's still a nice change to live out in the country.

Before going to work, to celebrate our first performance on our own without the Herods, Allene prepared a feast of cube steaks, mashed potatoes, and corn. Since my sister loves to cook, the three of us just let her. I helped by fixing lime Jell-O for dessert. The whole dinner was as good as a meal at Howard Johnson's! Even

Cheekaboom, whose favorite food is steak anyway, enjoyed the treat. Afterward, Peg and Penni volunteered to clear the table and do the dishes.

While putting on my stage makeup, I got to thinking about our situation. It seems funny to have Penni as our boss, and I wonder why the Herods picked her over Peg. Penni hasn't Peg's experience leading a chorus line, but on the other hand, she has a more bubbly, optimistic personality, which should be an asset when she's dealing with agents or managers. Plus, she owns the car. That counts.

I just wonder how Peg's taking the Herods' decision. I remember when she headed her own line of girls a couple of years ago. Every day she was busy fitting the dancers with costumes, rehearsing them with the music, and working on the choreography. The Herods set her up with all she needed, and Peg's group had solid bookings throughout the South and East. But it didn't last long. While doing clubs in New York, the girls got themselves rich boyfriends and staged a mutiny, leaving Peg high and dry. That really hurt her. She didn't even try to hire new girls. I remember, she called up the Herods and told them she was going home. They talked her into coming back with the revue. Peg's a great dancer and has always been a wonderful help to Betty with sewing costumes and training new girls as performers. Probably, Peg didn't want the job of leader again. Makes sense.

Had a good opening night show at the club. The music was fine, and the crowd liked our numbers. Best of all, the club manager looked pleased! But it sure seems different without the Herods. Now we simply do our dance routines at the beginning and end of each show, like any ordinary line of girls. There are no comedy skits or jokes like we did in the Manhattan Cocktail Revue, no solo routines for us, and no Jat or Betty around to handle show problems with music, lights, slippery floors, etc. Betty could fill in as one of the dancers, if needed, for any number, and Jat, on his violin, helped musicians immensely with tempos and melodies. Now, if something goes wrong, we have to wing it.

Our emcee is Cliff Winehill, a very funny man who looks a lot like Jimmy Durante, but with a cigar. He tells shaggy-dog-type stories or sings parodies of popular songs. Gets lots of laughs. But his Durante impersonation is what the audience waits to see. He can't help but go over big with that closer.

Also on the bill is a singer, Dorothy Miller, who sounds something like Georgia Gibbs. She does old favorites like George and Ira Gershwin's "Embraceable You." Dorothy has a great tan, and that's because, she told us, she plays golf every day at the country club across the road from the Pines. Tough life!

Wandered into the gambling room between shows and didn't see many customers at the tables or slot machines. It was very quiet, like no laughs or small talk allowed, just serious faces and hard concentration. The dealers seem amiable, but not inclined to talk much. And I noticed one of them looked like a chain smoker, with a cigarette stuck in the corner of his mouth like a permanent feature. Makes him look mean. The Humphrey Bogart look. Not that it matters.

I'm so glad the Manhattan Models got booked into Hot Springs and the Pines, instead of somewhere like Detroit and the Club 509, with its continuous shows, seven days a week. That's hard. This is much easier: two shows a night, six nights a week. But I sure miss the Herods.

March 1, 1955

Allene and I bleached one another's hair roots today, and something alarming happened: our bangs turned red. Although the rest of our hair turned blonde, as expected, our bangs with the new permanent became a sensational, fiery red! We washed our hair over and over, but it didn't do a bit of good. The red bangs stayed red. Peg suggested we use perfume for the horrible smell, so we sprayed Tigress cologne all over the top of our heads and opened the windows wide. Allene and I now have hair that is blonde in the back and red in the front, and there doesn't seem to be anything we can do about it. Wonderful.

After lunch, the four of us drove to downtown Hot Springs to check it out. Saw the popular mineral baths all in a row on one side of the main street and shops on the other. That's about it. Kind of a strange-looking, funny old town with its beneficial spas, like no place I've ever been. People come here from all over the country to cure their ills. It would be interesting to take walks around town every day, but we live too far out and can only come into town when Penni does.

We did go into a beauty shop to see what, if anything, the beautician could do about our hair. She cut off a piece of my bangs and put it in a glass with some hair bleach and said, "Check back in an hour." Unfortunately, there was no change!

Enjoyed a nice crowd at the club, and while the first show, where we do the Beach and the Gypsy, went fine, Allene and Peg had trouble in the second during the Cakewalk. Although it's one of our shortest numbers, the Cakewalk is exhausting because the whole routine is kicking, skipping, and hopping with canes. We wear lots of ruffles à la cancan dancers, and, for the finale, pull ribbon streamers from the back of one another's costumes. As might be expected, this dance lends itself to disasters: tangled streamers, dropped canes, and like what happened last night. My sister got her foot hung up in a ruffled petticoat and hopped around like she was in a one-legged race before she broke loose. Then Peg, at about the same time, grabbed her ruffled skirt instead of her foot for a leg stretch, and ripped it wide open. Not gently either, but all at once with a loud *RRRIP*. I did my best not to laugh.

Between shows tonight, I learned how to gamble. I had just been standing by the table watching when a small man with a big mustache gave me some chips and told me to place them on "No Pass." He said to just leave them there, so I did for a few throws of the dice. But as the pile of chips grew, I was too nervous to leave it all. (Guess I'm not a gambler!) I kept the bets small but still wound up winning $30. My friend said I could keep the money. I really like this place.

March 3, 1955

The four of us went to Oaklawn Racetrack this morning to check it out. Just like in the movies, there was a big grandstand, an oval track with a white fence all the way around, and scads of noisy people lined up at windows placing bets. Found space at the railing and cheered the horses running by, but noticed that the races seemed pretty short. Before you know it, it's all over and everyone hurries back and gets in line to bet again.

Watching the horses run, I was reminded of a story I read about Man ó War and why he was such a special racehorse. I went to the paddock between races, looking for an animal like him, that is to say, a horse that "measured up" as far as hands high and neck length. And I found one! While I got all excited over the similar statistics, Allene, Peg, and Penni looked at me like I'd lost my mind. According to the program, this horse had odds of twenty-two to one! Having no plans to spend money betting, I hurried back to the railing for the next race just to see if I'd picked a winner.

Well, there I was watching horses enter the track when a very drunk man in a loud flowered shirt came by and asked, in a heavy slur, if he could buy me a drink. I said, rather crisply, "No, thank you, but I'll take the two bucks you would spend for a highball." Weaving from side to side, the woozy stranger looked puzzled for a moment. Then, he fumbled in his pockets, pulled out two bills, and slapped them in my hand. I thanked him, ran off, and placed my bet, then stood at the rail to watch my horse win by two lengths! I went home $44 richer. I sure like Hot Springs.

Stopped at Kroger to pick up a few items, then drove back to the cabin with plans to rehearse over at the club in the afternoon. Penni told Peg to begin teaching Allene and me a new dance routine, while she made a trip to the Railway Express to pick up some wardrobe sent to us from Chicago by our agent. In case we're held over, we'll need to be up on plenty of numbers, so need to get prepared. Our rehearsal with Peg was to start at three o'clock. Allene and I went over to the club at two o'clock to run through the new numbers Betty had created for our singing act. Practiced a good hour and a half then sat down at one of the ringside tables and waited for Peg to come. Half an hour went by. No Peg. It was now almost four thirty. Just as we got up to leave, there came Peg all out of breath. It seems she was cornered by a huge spider! Afraid it might jump on her, she had inched her way across the front room to the kitchen where she grabbed the broom. Took her an hour, Peg said, but she finally managed to prod the thing out of the cabin. Glad I didn't see it!

Her spider adventure behind her, Peg got down to business. Started working on the routine for Look Out Jack, based on music

Jat wrote. Peg ran through it, humming the melody as she danced so we'd get a feel for the number. It's a modern jazz routine where we'll do knee drops, slides, jumps, and fast turns. Confirming our fears, it is a strenuous number. Allene and I will need to practice the individual steps and get them smooth before even trying to learn the whole routine. Grim. Ran through other line numbers we haven't done in a long time. Peg rehearsed the Blues, Samba, and Oriental, correcting our timing and any other sloppiness. She's very exact and is such a good dancer. I really admire her. Peg just breezes through everything with no fuss, no strain.

Today, when we returned to the cabin after rehearsal, Penni told the three of us that our contract's been extended. We're booked at the Pines Supper Club until March 18, at least. We must change shows every two weeks, though, so depending on how long we stay, plenty of costumes and dance routines must be ready for performance. Good thing Penni got Peg started on brushing up the line's repertoire.

Enormous crowd at the club tonight. Overheard several people saying they had come to the Pines Supper Club to see the cute little blondes with the curly red bangs. Allene and I are helping to draw in the crowds with this unexpected and surprising gimmick!

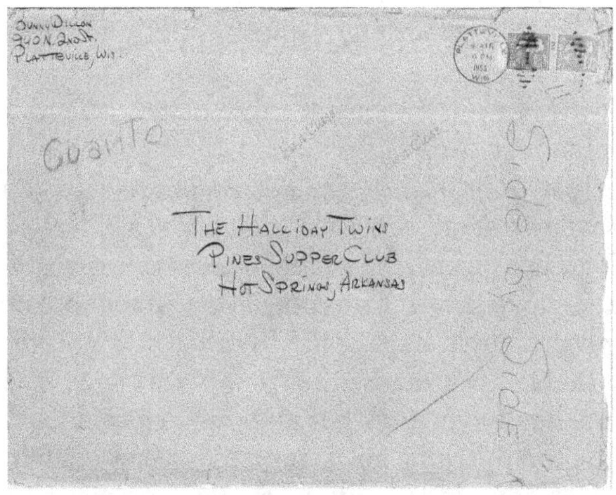

Getting mail at The Pines Supper Club, March 1955.

Penni filling water bottle at spring in Hot Springs, Arkansas, May 1955.

Chapter Seven

March 7, 1955

Drove into town this morning with Peg and Penni, who must see a dentist. Their teeth are turning black! Allene and I still have normal white teeth, so we think the problem is that Peg and Penni smoke, and whatever's in our water reacts to the nicotine. (The cabin water strikes again!) Anyway, they've got to get all the black scraped off. Lovely.

While we waited, Allene and I went to the post office to pick up mail and send money home. According to my ledger, we have sent $990 toward the house Mom and Papa are buying and redoing. Allene picked up letters from Tom, Francis, Paul, Jim, and Don. Nothing from Dick. Walked over to Kroger after that—a long walk. As planned, Peg and Penni met us there. The dentist's advice to them was to drink spring water.

Back home again, the four of us went to the club to rehearse the numbers for next week's change of show: Charleston, Samba, Oriental, and Hula. Spent hours going over and over the dances, mainly figuring out ways to get around Betty's part in the Charleston. Rather than change the music, one or all of us dances her part now. Good thing the club's air-conditioned because it was a pretty warm day. Our cabin was like an oven when we returned.

Since we're now twins, today is both Allene's and my birthday. We are supposedly twenty-three years old. We don't do much celebrating, so were pleasantly surprised when, between shows, we received a five-pound box of chocolates from the club owners, Mr. and Mrs. MacDonald, plus flowers from the Stangers, and a big ice cream cake from Peg and Penni. Super! Gave most of the cake and candy to employees at the club—the dealers, waitresses, and band members— so it was like a party for everyone. Allene was very good and didn't eat any of the desserts. She's still on the diet, eating mainly cottage cheese and fruit. Of course, I am too, but we're down to 112, so I had some birthday cake for both of us. Almost forgot. When we came into the club this evening there was a telegram from Dick to wish the TWO of us a happy birthday. Neat.

Met a bizarre character tonight who wanted to buy Allene and me a drink for our special day. He wore a crimson-red suit, purple shirt, and red tie. The outfit was topped off with a purple band on a red hat, as well as red shoes and socks. To attract further attention, he talked loudly and waved his hands around. Anyway, we ordered screwdrivers to make him happy, but when the waitress brought our beverages, this guy insisted on tasting one of them. I'm pretty sure he figured we were getting b-drinks—meaning the bartender wasn't putting in any alcohol. Well, it was so funny. While I sat with my mouth open at his rudeness, my sister, who had not yet mixed the orange juice on the bottom with the vodka on the top, right away handed this guy her drink. He took a gulp of pure vodka and started coughing. Ha! His face turned the color of his suit. "My God," he sputtered, "you gals sure can drink!" Serves him right.

March 11, 1955

It's another sunny, warm day, so Allene and I went out to sunbathe and write letters. We wore the bikinis we bought in Miami and spread out towels behind the club so no one would see or bother us. Allene wrote Mom, the Herods, Tom, Cal, Paul, and the Bryants. I'd planned to write too, but it was so nice and quiet and warm that I dozed off with my face on the stationery.

I don't know where she got the idea, but my sister thinks I need a high school diploma. Could be the Spanish book we bought in Lincoln with its "Easy as 1-2-3" language lessons. Or maybe Aunt Jean in Miami? Allene says I should make the most of our Hot

Springs engagement by getting educated. If we buy a correspondence course, I can go at my own pace and finish in no time, she thinks. Anyway, my sister has gone ahead and asked Mom to get info on the Calvert School (the same outfit Betty uses to teach JoAleene) and send it here. Humph.

Went into town with Peg and Penni around noon to get some groceries at Kroger and mail our letters. Did some shopping for other things too. Allene and I bought cute black and gold cocktail dresses at Mengal's and straw purses at the drugstore.

Hot Springs seems to be such a pretty place to live and work, a combination health spa and resort, with people coming as much for the mineral baths as for golf, gambling, or horse racing. Adding to the area's attributes is the clean, fresh spring water that flows constantly from a downtown fountain. Kind of neat. Thanks to the MacDonalds, the four of us have some large jugs and bottles we can fill with this special water. Too bad we didn't know about it before.

While in town, Peg bought a book all about spiders: the varieties, their mating habits, what they eat, types of webs, everything. Knowing more about the eight-legged critters, she thinks, will help her stay calm when one crosses her path or dangles from the ceiling. I figure it depends on their size.

Went to band rehearsal later today as we're changing shows. We have a new singer, Gloria, who is quite lovely, extra nice, and does a classy act too. One number she warbles without any musical accompaniment for several bars and, when the band does come in, she is right on key. Allene has determined that Gloria gets her starting note from the ending note of the previous song. It takes terrific concentration but it's too chancy, I'd say. Plus, I don't think an audience really appreciates that kind of skill. Maybe they do.

Great crowd tonight for the new lineup at the club. Since I'm behind on beading, I had planned to do some sewing between shows in the dressing room, but changed my mind and went out to mingle with the group. Met singer Jimmy Dean, who was in the audience. What a charmer! Very pleasant, yet not overly so. He truly enjoys people and has this wonderful southern drawl that makes him all the cuter.

Went into the casino to see who was there. An older gentleman who was losing walked away leaving me his chips, so I rolled dice for a while and won $10. Played blackjack after that and lost it all. Max, the dealer, was understanding and patient (even if it did take me forever to figure out what to do), telling me when to hit, when to stay, and how much to bet. This really is more fun than sewing beads in the dressing room.

Tonight, for her spot in the second show, Gloria wore a sensational floor-length, solid (almost) rhinestone sheath dress which glitters so much onstage in the spotlight, it almost hurts your eyes. Offstage and up close in the dressing room we share, I could see the heavy, canvas-type fabric the dress is made of to handle the weight of several thousand rhinestones. Anyway, most people hang up their costumes when they change, but Gloria took off the gown, threw it in a sack, and left it on the floor! I tried lifting that sack. It weighed a ton! I don't see how she can even wear that gorgeous gown without collapsing. For sure, no clothes hanger could hold that dress.

March 13, 1955

Peg received a phone call from Red yesterday, and they talked for a long time. When she finally hung up, our dancing buddy and roommate started to cry. Pretty dismal. Feeling low, Peg didn't eat much for dinner. The four of us went to work as usual, but between shows Peg started downing drinks, and by the end of the evening was totally smashed. Waving her arms around and giggling, she left the club after the last show and didn't get home until about noon today, dropped off at the cabin by some stranger. Who knows where she was? It's a worry when Peg goes off the deep end and doesn't know what she's doing. Once, she got so drunk after a show, she fell down a hill and broke her arm! The Herods stayed pretty calm considering they had to find a replacement fast. Penni knows Peg better than Allene and I do. They both had the same dancing teacher in Seattle and have worked with the Herods a year longer than we have. But, as close as they are, even Penni can't handle Peg if she's determined to binge.

The three of us went out for the day so Peg could sleep. We'd been invited to Frank and John's cabin on a lake. They're two very nice dealers who work the tables in Hot Springs each spring and then spend the rest of their time as part of a Las Vegas operation. Spent a quiet afternoon doing just about anything we wanted, like trying to catch a fish. Had a wonderful time but got nowhere with that, so went hiking in nearby woods. What a great place to live! Johnny cooked a terrific steak dinner, then, since this was everybody's day off, the five of us drove into Hot Springs to see *20,000 Leagues Under the Sea* at the movies.

Came home around midnight and went to bed. Early in the morning, Allene and I were suddenly awakened by rumbling thunder and spectacular lightning bolts—like the storm was right upon us! Next came the pounding rain, just pouring down. Cheeka yelped and went for cover under the bed. I pulled the blankets over my head, but it was impossible to sleep. In fact, none of us could sleep. One by one, the four of us got up and went into the kitchen. Peg fixed herself a sandwich since she hadn't eaten in some time. She looked a bit weary, but more or less normal, as though nothing unusual happened two days ago. We didn't ask her anything. Anyway, until the storm died down a little, we sat around the table eating prunes and dates, talking about Hawaii and Red (of course), the Herods, and the prospect of going back home one of these days.

March 17, 1955

Drove into town with Peg and Penni this afternoon. Allene and I went to the post office to pick up mail and to send Mom another $150 toward the house. We bought groceries at Safeway and refilled our water jugs at the town's fountain. The spring water tastes a lot better than the cabin water but doesn't change the red-bangs situation. In fact, Allene and I bleached and washed our hair yesterday using only spring water, and the blonde looked blonder and the red, all the redder. However, Penni and Peg's black-teeth problem has not come back.

While in town, Peg bought a blue parakeet and named him Billy after her boyfriend, Red, whose real name is Bill. She brought her little treasure home in a cage, along with a book on parakeet care and a supply of bird food. Cheeka took one sniff at the new pet and walked away in disgust. Billy now sits in his cage on a table next to the couch and chirps every so often. Peg showed us one of the tricks Billy does. She gets close to his cage and talks softly, then gives a low whistle. Her feathered friend reacts by poking his head through the cage wire and giving her a kiss.

Allene read her mail. A letter from Jim said he really wanted to see her again, so was packing his bags and leaving for Hot Springs, planning to arrive sometime on March 17—like sometime today. And he did!

I answered a knock on the cabin door about dinnertime. Jim came bouncing in, saw my sister, and gave her a hug before shoving some flowers and a big box of chocolates into her arms. (She almost fell over backward!) Then, he just stood looking at her and grinning from ear to ear. Saying he still needed to find a motel, Jim left as quickly as he'd arrived. Just checking in, I guess. He looks about the same as he did last year, maybe a little balder.

Tonight, all slicked up in a blue suit, Allene's conscientious admirer came to the club and sat alone, in the back at the bar, to watch the first show. There really was nowhere else for Jim to sit because it's St. Patrick's Day and the Pines was packed with a huge, boisterous crowd.

Unfortunately, Jim left early between shows, before Allene had a chance to join him. Probably felt neglected. It's just as well. During the second show, Allene's bra strap broke during the Oriental, and her top started to slide down to her waist. People were laughing as she made a fast exit. I'm sure, shy as he is, Jim would have blushed and been more embarrassed than my sister.

That wasn't all that happened during the second show. Our piano player, who can only play by ear, messed up Gloria's special big finish arrangement to the song that supplied the opening note for the next song. Backstage, we heard it. The band had not given her the note she needed, so she began singing in the wrong key. Humiliated because she was off-key, Gloria stopped singing mid-phrase and hurried offstage. She ripped open the dressing room door and just stood there for a moment, her eyes like blazing balls of fire! We got out of her way fast. Slamming the door shut, Gloria began pacing back and forth, back and forth, muttering, tearing at her hair, fuming and sputtering. None of us said a word, but we sure felt sorry for her. I'm glad I'm not a singer.

Saw the pushy jerk who wore the red suit before. He came in tonight wearing a bright green suit, hat, socks, etc. for St. Patrick's Day and was the center of attention again. Since he was buying champagne, Allene and I sat down (at his insistence) to toast the Irish. We decided to tolerate his rudeness, crudeness, and swearing one more time. After all, tonight he was playing the "big spender." Pretty soon a very drunk woman came along, sat down, and helped herself to the champagne. She talked loudly, but our friend talked louder. Pretty soon they were shouting. Every time he swore, she yelled at him and chewed him out! It Looked like a fight might develop, so Allene and I left.

March 22, 1955

Jim came by about noon and took Allene to breakfast while I stayed at the cabin, working on Spanish lessons, translating, and conjugating. It's fun to do, but would be a whole lot easier if someone around here spoke the language. And, if Allene has her way, I'll be doing a lot more than Spanish lessons. She is more certain than ever that I need to work on getting a high school diploma and is gung ho about enrolling me in the Calvert Correspondence School. I suppose I *can* squeeze the lessons in between my bead sewing and Spanish. Humph.

Peg and Penni were busy at the cabin too. While Peg went outside with her spider book, Penni sat on the bed, still in her pajamas, writing letters. Our leader likes to have her bowl of Grape-Nuts for breakfast, then, like today, hop back into or onto the bed to write to all her boyfriends across the country. And that can take hours! As usual, her 45-rpm record player droned away through stacks of her favorites—stuff by Tony Bennett, The Four Freshmen, and Billy Eckstine. I'll bet she's got several hundred of those little records with the big holes.

When Allene got back, she said Jim took her to the Colony Café for breakfast and then for a long drive so they could talk. He asked her to marry him (again), and she said she'd think about it (again). When our contract in Hot Springs is finished, Jim said he wants my sister to visit him in St. Louis. An engagement ring will be waiting if she's interested. Jim already had his car packed, so was not planning to hang around, and I guess by now is on the highway to Missouri. He's a nice, patient person, but I don't think Allene really cares about Jim or going to St. Louis. She just doesn't want to hurt his feelings.

After work tonight, Gloria and friends from Dallas—Al, Greg, and Tom—took Allene and me to see a dancer named Sheila. A friend of a friend told Gloria that Sheila was an absolute, one-of-a-kind, must-see, combination Cyd Charisse and Martha Graham. With the aid of a map, the six of us set out to find Club 21 where she performed. The place turned out to be a tavern located at the end of a gravel road in the woods. Went inside the dimly lit establishment and settled into a booth near a jukebox, where we ordered drinks (Allene and I had orange juice) from a waitress strolling around barefoot in a tight red dress. After someone put money in the jukebox, our waitress, aka Sheila, put down her tray and went into action, slowly twisting and turning as if in a trance. From time to time, she'd stop and pose, lifting one flexed foot in the air, then tilting forward or backward, flicking a ponytail that dangled over one ear. Weird performance, but I had to admire her balance.

There was a smattering of applause, and Sheila went back to serving drinks. The show over, we talked a little with our three Texas escorts about Dallas and Abe's Colony Club, where the revue was booked two years ago. Jim and Tom seemed to know the place, so Allene mentioned the highlight of our engagement there—the night the club caught fire during the show.

Jat, unaware of anything happening, was in the midst of telling mother-in-law jokes when people in the audience began to get up and leave, one by one. Our boss thought, at first, he must have offended someone, but then he turned to see that smoke was pouring out of the club's kitchen! Because it's an upstairs nightclub, the situation at Abe's Colony Club was potentially disastrous, and, standing backstage waiting to be introduced, we heard our boss calmly advising everyone to leave. Each of us dancers, in our satin bikinis and picture hats, turned and made a run for it, grabbing up wardrobe, props, and clothes as we hurried down the only stairs to the parking lot. Betty was right behind us with Jat's very old and priceless violin, which, in all the excitement, he forgot! Not much damage to the club (beyond the kitchen) except a lingering smoky smell.

The other exciting, newsworthy event was that there was a nude prowler going around in the area. Apparently, he didn't steal anything or hurt anyone. He'd just show up, unannounced and uninvited, in somebody's living room buff naked. This was alarming enough to cause an uproar in the city as it occurred several times, and he hadn't been captured.

Allene and I were living in a separate motel cabin from Penni and Peg, as well as from the Herods in Dallas. Since the motel had a park-like setting with plenty of trees between the individual cabins, it was spooky at night. So, being nervous, we started bringing home our metal batons from the football routine after work as protection in case we were visited by the prowler.

One night after the Herods had dropped us off at our cabin, we heard a rustling noise coming from the kitchen. Immediately, we thought of the prowler. Creeping softly over to the doorway, we peeked in and saw torn wrappers and broken crackers on the floor. The prowler was hungry. Allene bravely stepped into the kitchen with me close behind, both of us hanging onto our batons ready to attack, AND found a mouse frantically trying to get behind the stove by going between it and the wall. Breathing sighs of relief, we managed to get this very frightened prowler into a wastebasket and out the backdoor!

Manhattan Cocktail Revue poster from 1955.

Betty and Jat Herod, 1955.

Chapter Eight

March 24, 1955

Jim called from St. Louis to talk to Allene. My sister was pleasant but not encouraging over the phone, and I think he got the message. Too bad. I wonder if we'll see him again. After that, Penni got a call from the Herods in England telling her to be sure to pay their taxes for them. They said Scotland was wet, grey, and dismal all the time. The food wasn't any good, and they can't wait to get back home! But JoAleene did manage to buy some new genuine puppets for her Zany Puppet Show.

Jat is playing theaters in the London area now. He said vaudeville is still going strong in England, with lots of variety acts touring the country, working regular theater circuits. So far, Jat has been booked with acrobats, jugglers, magicians, ventriloquists, and trained dogs. The acts, he said, move around doing two-week engagements, two shows a day. They must live in theatrical boarding houses called digs, which are cold and awful, but that's what everyone does. It's a whole different scene compared with show biz in this country, but probably not unlike the way things were here thirty years ago.

Allene and I rehearsed at the club with Peg and Penni to get routines ready for another show change. Worked on Look Out Jack again. I really like the music, a combination of tunes Jat wrote with jazzy lyrics from the bebop era, but the choreography is difficult. In fact, I almost dread what I know I have to do! Peg and Penni are strong dancers and look so good zipping around, doing the jumps, splits, and knee slides. We try, but Allene and I are picking up more bruises than dance steps. And we're not even up to tempo yet.

Another number we practiced today is a new Gypsy routine with tambourines. Not much different from the old Gypsy routine except we whirl all over the place barefoot in costumes made of little more than floor-length colored ribbons. After that, we reviewed dance numbers like the Mambo, the Hoedown, and Babalu (an Afro-Cuban number based on the song written by Margarita Lecuona) where Peg, Penni, and Allene dance around in sarongs clutching trays of flowers on their heads. Then, I come out for a sexy solo part, slinking around in a white feathered and rhinestone outfit. The costume had to be taken in because I am not as buxom as Madelaine, the original dancer for this solo. I never met her but have seen her show photos that were taken a few years ago. She could have given Marilyn Monroe a run for her money. I like Babalu mainly because I don't have to wear shoes. Anyway, we concentrated on placement in these routines and really got a good workout—sore muscles too.

Penni and Allene drove into town to fill the water jugs and pick up the mail while Peg and I stayed at the cabin. For the most part, Peg read one of her spider books. She has three now plus a magnifying glass, so has become quite an expert, we think. Since we live in a region full of crawly things, she's got lots of specimens she can examine close up. Lately, she's tried to figure out what kind of spider lives behind the refrigerator. He isn't very cooperative, though, and scoots underneath the drip pan when Peg gets too close. She tries to find him with a flashlight, but he manages to disappear into a crack or behind something.

I spent a couple of hours listening to Penni's records while sewing on our new Mexican Hat Dance skirts. They are made from a heavy cotton material Allene and I bought in Juarez when we were there a couple of years ago. It is stamped with large, brightly colored sombreros, cacti, and flowers. The plan is to outline each, then fill them solid with beads of various colors. Should look beautiful, but one bead at a time takes forever. By the time I finish, I'll be too old to do the number!

Thanks to me and my mouth, Peg came up with a money-saving plan. I accidentally jabbed my thumb with the needle and yelled, "Damn!" A minute later I spilled a bag of beads across the floor and swore again. Peg started to laugh and said what we need around here is a cuss box. If anyone swears it should cost them a nickel a word. She then found an ashtray, labeled it "Cuss Box," and held out her hand, waiting for my dime. I gave her a quarter instead just to kind of kick things off.

Practiced a little bit with Cheekaboom after that. I've started training her, so she'll know a trick or two to show off like Billy the bird. She's a pretty smart little dog if you can get her attention. Anyway, this is the routine we rehearse: Instead of just picking her up as usual, with two hands, I say, "Get on the elevator" and reach for her with my right palm open. She walks onto it and is so small she straddles my hand from my fingers to my wrist. Then, I lift her up. Simple. Except if Cheeka gets excited and starts wiggling around, it's no use.

It's too bad Cheeka isn't a bigger pooch. Then, we could develop something more impressive, like the old vaudeville routine where a woman comes onstage wearing a fur piece around her neck. First, she adjusts it across her shoulders, then drapes it over one arm, and finally sets it on the floor where it becomes a dog that runs off stage. Terrific trick! Tonight, between shows, Mr. Stanger gave a surprise birthday party for our emcee, Cliff Winehill, who has come back for another two-week engagement. Cliff was really delighted. He gave a little speech and made a wish that he'd be here at the Pines to celebrate his next birthday. Then, he blew out the one candle on his cake. (No one knows for sure how old he is.) Everybody in the club, customers and all, were invited to have some of the huge birthday cake. Peg, Penni, Allene, and I knew about the party ahead of time, so bought Cliff silver cufflinks and a giant cigar to use in his act. That really cracked him up. Mrs. Stanger was at the party, carrying her little white poodle, this time both wearing matching bright blue ribbons with blue rhinestone chokers. Stole the scene, of course.

Later, talked with some gamblers in the casino who worked at the Wort Hotel in Jackson Hole last year when we appeared there. I don't remember them, but they saw the Manhattan Cocktail Revue every night for a week. Seems we were an exception at the Wort because we didn't do Western stuff. I remember we *did* feel out of place. Everything around us had to do with cattle or cowboys. There was a gambling room at the hotel that I liked to go into between shows to watch fellows playing poker. That could get pretty exciting when lots of money was at stake. The spectacular Silver Dollar Bar in the saloon is famous. Jackson Hole is still the Old West.

Also tonight, while in the casino, I met Tom and Leo at the roulette table. They're business partners who raise horses in Tennessee most of the year, then come to Hot Springs each spring to gamble and play golf. Tom and Leo treated the four of us to champagne between shows and, after work, to barbecued ribs at a restaurant downtown. Very nice guys. I wanted to talk about horse racing and the Oaklawn racetrack, but they didn't seem interested in discussing horses. Just golf and boats.

March 29, 1955

Last night, Penni got some free tickets to Oaklawn; therefore, this morning we went to the races. Our box seats, in the grandstand where we had an unobstructed view of the racetrack, were really good. But it was all enclosed and smoky. After a few minutes, Allene and I made our way outside to breathe clean air. We stood by the rail, like before, to watch the races, and overheard a racetrack gag: "Went to the track the other day and met a lady with a box seat," one fellow commented. "Yeh?" his friend responded. "Yeh, but she wore a long jacket that covered it nicely." Ha! Saw the same drunk in the flowered shirt who gave me $2 last time we were here, but he didn't recognize me. GOOD.

Strolled over to the paddock like last time but couldn't find a horse that "measured up," so I wasn't interested in betting. However, Peg and Penni, feeling kind of reckless, decided to give it a whirl and lost their money. Time to leave! We had to get back for an afternoon band rehearsal at the club anyway. We're changing shows again.

Dorothy Miller, the singer-golfer, is back, and our emcee is now Allen Reno, a very amiable fellow who comes onstage wearing a baggy suit and dilapidated hat with a daisy on it. Right after we open the second show with the Mambo in our tight white costumes with big, ruffly sleeves, he launches into a bunch of city-slicker-in-the-country jokes. Allen's five-minute routine gives Peg and Penni time to change into little soldier outfits with lots of leg showing for a military tap. The dance is loaded with drumrolls and precision tapping, very straight and stiff, like an army rifle drill. Peg and Penni are absolutely together! The only thing missing which could make the routine tighter and better is Joann, our friend in Indiana. She was a really sharp tap dancer.

Other show changes included the new Gypsy with all the colored ribbons and the Hoedown. Allen Reno plays fiddle, so he joined us, like Jat, playing the "Chicken Reel," and making the Hoedown more of a country square dance. Having a foot-stomping fiddler adds to the number, that's for sure.

Between shows I had great fun watching gamblers roll the dice at one of the tables. It was pretty exciting to see all those chips being pushed around after each roll of the dice. Stood next to a nice-looking, middle-aged man who seemed to know what he was doing. His name was Roy, and he came from Little Rock. He won consistently in the dice game. I think Skeets, the dealer, was happy to see him move over to the roulette wheel. I went with him (kind of liked this guy). He told me he'd run a club in Reno before moving to Arkansas and advised me that if I wanted to be lucky at gambling, I'd have to watch carefully and remember the numbers coming up. Roy won at roulette too but didn't get one bit excited about his winning streak. In fact, he seemed bored. Because he acted like such a cool character who always wins, I think he must be very confident or have lots of money to burn. Or both. He didn't stay to see our second show, so maybe I bored him too.

While I was with Roy, Allene amused herself at the dice game table, shuffling chips with one hand, like the dealers do, and she's getting pretty good at it. Skeets and the other dealers get a kick out of her accomplishment. Developing nimble fingers seems more interesting to my sister than gambling.

Big surprise! Ross Russell, our Atlanta agent, came to see our first show. He talked to Penni and hinted we may get a booking in Atlanta after here. Having only met him one other time, I didn't even recognize the man sitting ringside. (Just as well. If I'd known he was in the audience, I'd have loused up for sure.) Ross said the Manhattan Models were looking good and that Mr. Stanger was quite pleased with our routines and performances. Then, he asked about the Herods since he hadn't heard from them. He left after that.

"On the Road to Mandalay," based on Rudyard Kipling's poem, is our closer for the second show this week. The band is still struggling a bit with the music, but it should improve. Allene does Betty Herod's singing part in this Middle Eastern harem number, then joins us for the dance. Guess it was my turn to have costume trouble. If it weren't for the finger cymbals we use, I could have stopped my pants zipper when it started to come apart. There I was with the bottom half of my costume falling off and grabbing at the material with clanking cymbals, attracting attention to my problem. I stayed and finished the dance using the big veil attached to my hat to cover my rear end, but I could hear people laughing. Oh well. It could have been worse.

I noticed that the Pines Supper Club has installed a TV set over the bar. It seems dumb, but I think people want to just sit there with their drinks and watch sports. At least the bartender turns it off during the show!

March 31, 1955

Beautiful day, so all of us sunbathed behind the club. Went into town afterward and picked up mail from Bob, Steve, Jim, Francis, Don, and Mom, who writes she's been called back to work part time at J.C. Penney because they're busy and shorthanded for their Easter specials. She enclosed a very nice letter from Calvert School. Although they wrote they would send books and tests wherever we travel, their education package is a pretty expensive deal. Allene says she wants to think about it. Big Sister gave me a test on "Lesson 7" in the Spanish book, and I only missed two sentences. Spanish is fun to write, but I can't read aloud very well. Nothing with rolled RRRs comes out right, and if I try too hard blowing with my tongue against my teeth, I spit all over. Charming.

Allene and I took a long hike after that, walking about five miles out on a dirt road. Saw lots of lovely trees swaying in the breeze, heard birds chirping, and watched a shallow stream full of rocks rushing next to the road. It's wonderful to have all this so close to where we are staying, but kind of makes us homesick too. There are many areas around Anacortes or over on Guemes Island where a person can hike all day without seeing another person or hearing anything but insects buzzing and the sound of wind rushing through fir trees. And we miss that. Hot Springs is wonderful, though. We're lucky to be here. On days like today, I sure feel sorry for the people who have to live in cities.

Sometimes my big sister and I feel we simply must get out for fresh air. Between the club and the cabin, the air we breathe gets pretty stale with cigarette smoke. Allene becomes so annoyed when Peg and Penni are smoking that she throws open windows or closes the bedroom door. I'm sure our roommates get her message. But they pay half the rent, so they have their rights too. It's just that the tobacco smell is so powerful and lingering, it gets in our hair and clothes. I think people who smoke don't care about that or even notice the stink.

Came back home. Allene wrote Dick—he loves the outdoors too—while I tackled "Lesson 8" in the Spanish book. Got distracted when Peg let Billy out of his cage, and he flew all around the cabin. Cheeka ran behind the couch to hide! Usually, after his exercise, Billy ends up perched on the lampshade to rest his wings. Today, he sat on one of the bedposts. Doesn't seem interested in going outside, which is good.

Penni, Peg, Allene, and I are trying a new type of diet. Every other day we have boiled eggs and skim milk and nothing else. On days in between we can eat normally, but no ice cream, cake, or other bad things. Today, I ate two soft-boiled eggs and drank two glasses of skim milk. At the club in the evening, I had two more glasses of skim milk and was still hungry! Penni and Peg are drinking buttermilk instead of skim because it has more flavor (and calories, Allene says). Had to laugh, tonight at the end of the Gypsy, Penni turned the wrong way and ran right into Allene. I told her it must be the buttermilk.

Dorothy, our singer, has a bad cold so she did a really short spot tonight—and it was terrible. She started to sing "Little White Lies" and it came out sounding very hoarse and rough. Then, she started to cough. Pretty embarrassing for her. Good thing it was a slow night at the club. I played dice between shows because so few customers were around, then one of the dealers taught me how to play gin rummy.

Right after the last show, Peg and Penni were so hungry they drove downtown for barbecued ribs. So much for diets.

April 4, 1955

Allene and I got up early and went into town with Penni just before noon for a special reason. We had made an appointment at LaRay's beauty parlor downtown to see if someone there could bleach our hair into one color. Everyone in the shop seemed fascinated with the red-bangs problem and had to take an up-close look. None of the beauty operators had ever seen anything like it! Two gals went to work on our heads with bleach, concentrating on the bangs, and did their best. Although the rest of our hair is pale blonde now, the bangs are still stubbornly RED. Went to the post office. No mail today.

Peg and Penni went out to dinner at the Smorgasbord restaurant on the other side of town with Mr. Owens, the newspaperman. Allene and I could have gone too, but instead, stayed home and had our eggs and skim milk. I'm sure getting sick of eggs and skim milk, but it works. Weighed ourselves at the drugstore today, and we're down to 110! Besides, I wouldn't want Mr. Owens to pay for dinner for all of us, and I'm sure he would have. He's very pleasant, but I don't think he has a lot of money.

We see so much of Peg and Penni anyway; Allene and I would just as soon stay home and enjoy the quiet. This is the longest we've roomed with Peg and Penni. I'm afraid they just have different ways and can certainly do nerve-wracking things such as Peg cracking her knuckles and leaving her shoes on the coffee table, or Penni gritting her teeth when she washes dishes and buying cookies with raisins then picking them all out—which is strange considering she likes raisins straight out of a box.

But on the flip side of the situation, Allene aggravated Peg and Penni the other day when she spilled salt in the kitchen then threw some over her left shoulder for good luck. (I must admit, the floor got a little crunchy.) And Penni has complained more than once that she can't stand the scraping sound when I file my fingernails. Oh well, we're all saving money so better just put up and shut up all the way around.

Allene and I wore our brown print dresses with matching stoles to the club tonight and, boy, did we get the turned heads and whistles. The outfit only took about one day to make on our portable Singer machine. The material is beautiful. Next, we're planning to stitch up blue velveteen strapless cocktail dresses with silver-blue mink tails, which we can buy at $2 apiece from Dee Cross, our friend who works at the furrier in Dubuque, for trim across the top.

Part of the club was closed off and, even at that, the crowd was small (nice though). Business is definitely down. Could be because the racing season's over. Between shows, Allene and I went into the casino and played blackjack for fun with Skeets, one of the dealers. Three interesting gentlemen from Memphis—Don, Lee, and Bob—joined us. They are here for a telephone conference and to play golf for a few days. I asked about the Silver Slipper in Memphis where we worked two years ago, and they said it's definitely closed down. Too bad.

After trying their luck at roulette, the three decided all five of us should have steak and champagne dinners. (Yum.) Right away, Don took a liking to my big sister. He's blond and really cute and comes from Houston originally, so has a darling accent. Penni stopped by our table—all smiles, sweet, and charming—commenting on Don's cute accent and how much she loved to hear him talk. She sat down and had some champagne, which reminded me that our leader is not shy around handsome men with Southern accents or Western drawls. Based upon time spent around Penni and how she snares guys, I feel certain she has her eye on Don. Well, she'll have to pedal a little faster to keep up with my sister!

There's been a change in our show. Allen Reno left, and our singer friend Dorothy has been too sick to perform. Replacements are Bob Hannon, a singer from New York, and his wife, Rowena Rollins, a comedienne. Bob used to sing on the radio for *Manhattan Merry-Go-Round*, so Allene and I had heard him before. Never thought we'd be doing shows with him! I think he's great and told him so.

Rowena does a comedy skit, "Cooking with Sherry," which is very funny and plays something like this: A table of cooking props is onstage when Rowena comes out. She puts on an apron and begins a step-by-step cooking demonstration on how to bake a chicken. The recipe calls for sherry, which she nips on throughout the demonstration, explaining what she's doing while mixing ingredients in a bowl and getting progressively sloshed. Forgetting what she's doing, she giggles a lot and slaps the chicken around. Then, in the end, with the bird on the floor and the mixing bowl in the oven, she slurs, "I . . . *hic* . . . can't imagine why more . . . *hic* . . . people don't cook with sherry . . . *hic!*"

Another change: Buddy Blake sings with the band between shows, doing popular songs. He's from Hot Springs and has a nice smooth style, kind of like Frank Sinatra, but Buddy's a lot better looking. Also, the Manhattan Models are doing a different routine in the last show. The Blues replaces Road to Mandalay, which wasn't going over well, mainly because the band had nothing but trouble with the music. (If Jat were here with his violin, he could have kept them on course and up to tempo.) The new number uses "Blues in the Night," written by Harold Arlen and Johnny Mercer, a popular song I think all musicians know. To add time, Peg and Penni are doing a couple of duets where they're dancing on their toes much of the time. Not easy. Takes tough toes! And strong toe shoes.

By the time we got home tonight from the club, there was all kinds of thunder and lightning. Soon enough, the full storm hit with lots of wind and rain. Loud as it was, we managed to sleep through the racket until Allene and I were awakened by the sound of running water very close by. Too close by. Suddenly, water poured down the INSIDE of the venetian blind and onto the bed, splashing us from head to toe like there was no window there at all! Jumped up to avoid being drenched more, then, as fast as we could, pulled the bed away from the window. That done, we got dry blankets and fresh pajamas and went back to sleep.

April 6, 1955

Went into town this afternoon with Peg and Penni to fill the water jugs and go to the post office. Picked up letters from Ray, Dick, Francis, Don, and Sid. Then, it was over to Walgreens and Kress for cosmetic supplies. Drove from there to Railway Express where each of us sent our furs to Dee Cross for storage until winter. Penni sent her full-length, beige fur coat she fondly refers to as "Old Gamey." I don't know what kind of fur the coat is, but our leader certainly won't need anything that heavy until fall. Peg shipped her dark brown marmot jacket too. At least their furs are paid off. Allene and I still have one more payment to make on our mouton jackets before we own them completely. Then, there are our marmot stoles with mink tail trim which are more expensive and will take longer to pay off. Dee's nice about giving us extra time to settle the bill for those. The stoles we'll keep with us, but the jackets need to go to storage.

Today, our publicity man, Mr. Owens, stopped by. He's the one who's been creating half-page ads for the Pines Supper Club, showing the Manhattan Models, plus whatever acts are appearing with us. He brought the four of us some fresh bass he'd just caught. Fishing is tops around here at this time of the year. Apparently, Mr. Owens loves going out in his boat and dropping a line. Didn't take much to get him talking about it either. He got so excited discussing fishing holes and lures that his Adam's apple went up and down, up and down. I found it quite fascinating. Allene baked the bass for dinner, and it was really good.

Thrill of the day—Penni got a letter from Frank, her heartthrob. It had been several weeks since she'd heard from him, so she got all excited. Frank's in the air force, stationed in Albany, Georgia, and really good-looking, but he's engaged to a girl back home in New Jersey. Nonetheless, Penni loves him and he loves her, she claims. However, since Frank's parents are gung ho in favor of the impending marriage to the other girl, it seems our leader is beating her head against a brick wall. In their eyes, dancing girls just don't carry enough good credentials for their son. Reminds me of an old movie plot.

Penni also heard from the Herods who are still in England

and not very happy. They say they're freezing all the time. Can't get or stay warm when there is no central heating, just something called shilling meters which hardly do the job. Plus, the English meals continue to be exceedingly dull and disappointing. Breakfast consists of cold unbuttered toast and bitter coffee, and, if you'd like dinner at teatime, forget it. Not available. The Herods plan on sailing to New York in June and are really looking forward to getting back to the States. In July, Betty writes, the revue will do outdoor grandstand shows in Minnesota at small-town county fairs. We all said, "What?" So, Penni read that piece of news over again. I can't imagine us doing outdoor county fair shows since we always work in nightclubs, but it might be a nice change. Something new for the Manhattan Cocktail Revue.

Tonight, Don from Memphis came alone to the club to see Allene, and I noticed he had that look in his eye. Between shows the two had dinner by candlelight in a corner of the dining room. I think my sister likes him too. Saw Penni sitting at the bar alone, sipping a sloe gin fizz and kind of watching them.

Chapter Nine

April 15, 1955

One year ago today, the Manhattan Cocktail Revue opened at Leroy's in Honolulu for a four-month engagement. Leroy's was not a regular tourist club on the beach, but more of a hangout for Honolulu locals of many nationalities. The revue was a novelty there since we didn't perform the hula or sing Hawaiian songs. Also, except for Betty, all the Manhattan Models were blondes at that time. Penni, our redhead, had left the show to return to college and had been replaced by Madelaine's younger sister, Candy, who was also beautiful and buxom. We did two shows a night with an occasional extra show or commercial on KONA TV to advertise refrigerators. Kind of fun and new for us.

One day the four of us went deep-sea fishing with friends. The water was so rough, I couldn't stay inside the cabin because I felt seasick. Spent five hours clinging to a railing topside and got a terrible sunburn as a result, especially on my face, even though I wore a big, brimmed sunhat. Allene thinks it was the sun's reflection from the water on my face. All I know is that it sure hurt, and because of the blisters, I couldn't wear makeup from under my eyes down to my chin. Lovely. And I still had to work.

There were nicer things that happened during our stay, such as learning the authentic hula, how to eat with chopsticks, and touring the pineapple and sugarcane plantations. Also, we performed two very special shows for the lepers at Kalaupapa on Molokai. When the

Manhattan Cocktail Revue, with the band from Leroy's, arrived by plane to put on performances outside under palm trees and inside the hospital, it was the first time the residents had seen a show in ten years. We were treated royally and showered with special leis the lepers had made. Not a dry eye was to be found anywhere when these isolated people sang a Hawaiian farewell to us as we got back on the plane for Honolulu. Had to laugh, though, because Leroy's young vibraphone player, Arthur Lyman, looked scared to death when we took off. It seems he had never been on a plane before that day!

The most memorable event at Leroy's, for us, was the night the termites swarmed throughout the club. First, the manager turned off the club lights, hoping they'd be attracted to the streetlights outside. (They weren't.) Second, he turned on big fans to blow the bugs out of the open doors and windows. (Didn't help a bit.) Showtime! As soon as the music began and we dancers reached the well-lit stage, termites were on us, flying into our faces and crawling all over our arms and necks. They were in our mouths and on our teeth. I think I spent more time swatting than dancing! Hazards of entertainment in the tropics. Termite night in Honolulu!

Candy didn't stay with the revue long. A handsome sailor stationed in Honolulu swept her off her feet, and she married him in July. Fortunately, Penni had had enough of college by then, so she rejoined us in time to attend the big wedding.

So much for the good old days, one year ago in Honolulu. Of course, Peg is feeling sentimental since that's where she met Red, the love of her life. She has just finished writing him a long letter that's taken her three days to complete.

This morning the four of us went out to Lake Hamilton near Hot Springs to sunbathe, play catch, and ride around in a speedboat. Jack, one of the managers of the club, and his wife wanted us to relax and have a good time at their home on the water. We sure did. Such nice people! When it was lunchtime, Jack fixed huge, terrific barbecued burgers. Each of us took some leftover meat for Cheeka. She's got enough to last several days, for sure.

Back at our cabin, getting ready for work, Peg let Billy out to fly around while she put on her stage makeup. He landed on her head instead of the lampshade. (Cute trick if you like birds!) Seeing Billy in the mirror, standing in her blonde curls, Peg was so shocked and surprised that she dropped her face powder right down the sink. Kind of a mess. Mischief mission completed, Billy flew over to his usual roost on the lampshade.

Bob Hannon and Rowena Rollins, our good friends, closed tonight. They are so full of fun I know we're going to miss them. After Rowena finished her "Cooking with Sherry" routine, she surprised the four of us by prancing onstage behind us during our blues number. We kept moving, but it was hard not to glance at her and laugh. There she was, a fifth Manhattan Model, dancing all over the place and doing a great job too. We figured she must have been watching us from backstage every night.

April 20, 1955

Weather has been very warm, but cloudy like it might rain. Lots of bugs are coming out now, and some are weird looking too. Every day, when one of us first opens the front door, she finds dead beetles all over the cement entry step. Some even fall inside the cabin. Then, at night, when we have the bathroom light on, you can hear flying things banging themselves on the window, like someone throwing rocks at the side of the cabin.

Mom wrote that the house and renovations are coming along okay, but not fast enough. Sounds like she's really putting in a colorful garden and making the most of old things lying around the property, like vintage wheelbarrows and wagon spokes, that make for an interesting yard. She's thinking of getting Mr. Lowman, the stonemason, to replace part of a wall in the front room with a big stone fireplace. And Papa got some knotty pine boards to lighten up the living and dining rooms. Can't wait to see the place! Late this afternoon, Mr. Owens stopped by to bring us some more fish. It's called croppie. Our good friend looked a bit sunbaked but happy, like he'd been out on the water all day. I wonder when he finds time to do his newspaper work. Anyway, now I know what a croppie looks like. Allene baked the fish, and it was delicious with lemon.

We've changed shows again. Penni is hauling out every dance

routine she can think of. Lots of rehearsals coming up.

In the second show, I lost a shoe doing my solo in the Oriental number. When Allene started singing, I accidentally kicked it off— all the way across the stage! That's because the shoes that match the costume are Betty's and are too big for me. Everyone in the audience started laughing while I hopped around, trying to pick up the shoe and get it back on. Oh well. Then, to top things off, all the lights went out in the club for about an hour because of an electrical storm.

April 23, 1955

Weather is really hot now. Heat bugs buzz, and the air doesn't seem to move. To funnel any breezes through the cabin, we have doors and windows wide open, and that helps a little. Poor Cheeka lies sprawled out on the kitchen linoleum most of the time now instead of the bed. Since the four of us are roasting from morning until evening, we wear our bathing suits all day trying to stay cool. But running around in a bikini really doesn't solve the heat problem since so much skin is exposed. If you sit on a hot chair with bare legs, it's like getting burned on a stove.

Drove into town to fill our water jugs and go to the post office. Allene and I sent more money home for the house. Total is now about $1,200.

Peg got a phone call from Red this afternoon. He is home in California now, out of the Navy, coming to see her and arriving sometime this week. Boy, is Peg excited! It is Red's birthday in a couple of days, so she went ahead and ordered him an ice cream cake. Then, because she wants to look her best (of course), I helped her bleach her hair today. And wouldn't you know it, that darn Billy tried to land on her head when it was full of foam! To make sure she looks like a movie star, Peg's sewing up a powder blue, strapless cocktail dress with blue sequins. She's hurrying to finish so she can wear it to the club that special day Red arrives. Peg looks sensational in the gown because it really shows off her blue eyes and big bust.

Today, Mr. MacDonald cut the grass away from around our cabin and the club, hoping, he says, to reduce the huge quantity of bugs and spiders living here. I think he may be too late. We seem to have quite an assortment. Fortunately, crawly things don't bother Peg now. Last week, using one of her books, she identified a pregnant spider and watched it daily until hundreds of baby spiders hatched just outside the kitchen window. Pretty soon the mother spider left, and the little ones scattered or got eaten by something. Now Peg is regularly inspecting another type of spider, kind of beige and hairy, that has built a magnificent web between two bushes. The one behind the refrigerator left.

Mr. Owens stopped by with some more fish. I don't know what it is—but Allene baked it. Seems to me the four of us should invite Mr. Owens to stay for dinner sometime since he's been so generous. Our publicity man is too shy to even hint he's tired of being alone and fixing fish for himself. That's what I think, anyway.

The show is quite long this week. Kalantan, an exotic dancer from Las Vegas, is on the bill with us now. She's a beautiful brunette, kind of on the small side, and her act is unusually good. Some of what she does is like belly dancing, I'd say, with the shimmies and undulations. When she first comes onstage, Kalantan dances to Yma Sumac's exotic style of music and then switches to drums alone. Our drummer really likes that part. Gives him a chance to do some special stuff like extended loud then soft, wave-like drum rolls. And, of course, he must watch Kalantan closely to accent her every wiggle with a rim shot or cymbal crash. I think he's having the time of his life!

Cliff Winehill, who is a great favorite here, opens this Friday. The four of us look forward to seeing him again. Then, singer Brenda Hollis begins on the following Monday. She has already arrived and moved into the cabin next to ours. Seems pleasant and, Allene guesses from Brenda's comments, that she is a vegetarian. I hope she doesn't mind all the bugs and spiders.

May 4, 1955

Red came last week and is staying with the four of us in the cabin. Peg asked Penni, Allene, and me ahead of time how we'd feel about that. We said we could manage one extra person for a short stint. Just out of the Navy, Red hasn't a job or much money. Peg didn't know how long he would be in Hot Springs or if he would remain at all. She just wanted to see and be with him again. Anyway, Red's sleeping in the living room on the couch, and it's a good thing he isn't any taller than six feet because he just fits! So far, his presence has not caused even one problem. It's a nice novelty to have a visitor here, especially someone like Red who is more like having a brother around. Nothing seems to bother him, such as contending with the hand-washed underwear of four females that hangs to dry, day after day, on every doorknob and coat hook or across the shower rod; needing to wait in line to use the bathroom; having space on the sink or in the cabinet for his shaving stuff; and trying to find room in the refrigerator for his beer. Red takes it all in stride and kind of fits right in. He's polite and considerate and laughs easily too. I can see why Peg is crazy about him.

Earlier, Peg showed Red Billy's cute trick with the kiss through the birdcage, and today our houseguest tried it. Red talked softly then whistled low and even. The little bird cocked his blue feathered head from side to side like he was listening. Then, he poked it through the wires to give Red a kiss—and got stuck! All puffed up and squawking, Billy pushed with his feet and twisted his head around like crazy. We hurried out of the room, hoping the bird would calm down and back out. Didn't work. Red had to force the wires apart.

I wonder what the Herods would say about Red's being here. This situation is so funny considering the way Betty preaches to every girl who joins the revue about her rules regarding a dancer's behavior, offstage as well as on. Besides a glamourous appearance and good manners, there was the matter of appropriate conduct in all instances, especially those having to do with men. One slipup, one indiscretion, could tarnish the reputation of the whole revue. Concerning males, we were never to leave a club alone with one and, under no circumstances, could a man enter your hotel or motel room. Shoot, now we've got one living with us.

However, Red will leave soon, driving first to San Antonio where he'll pick up his folks, then it's on to his home in Merced, California. After that, Red plans to return to Hot Springs. I know Peg is going to miss him. They are together all the time, going off every day after breakfast, driving "wherever the car takes them," Peg says. Red comes to the club every night too. Looks serious, but Peg tells us she won't marry Red until he finds a job. She promised her parents she would not do anything rash or foolish. Uh-huh.

Today, Allene and I bleached our hair and left the smelly foam on for one whole hour. Now our bangs are dark orange. It's a wonder our hair hasn't just plain fallen out! Each of us now has about one and a half inches of bleached blonde under orange, frizzy bangs. Oh boy.

Picked up letters from Captain Bryant, Cal, Ray, and Dick, who writes that he and his friend, Dave, are opening a hot dog stand in Jackson Hole soon. Sounds like fun. At last, Dick is out of Los Angeles and living where he really prefers to be. He thinks Jackson Hole is the place to be now that Rockefeller's big resort is finished, which should bring lots of tourists to the area. Allene cannot imagine Dick wearing a cap and apron, cooking hot dogs for a living. I have to agree it's strange. Maybe this was friend Dave's idea.

The Herods sent Penni a box of souvenirs including French Line menus, silk scarves, heather soaps, and assorted coins from England and France for all of us, as well as a message saying they are excited about sailing to New York on June 14 aboard the *Île de France*. After arriving, they go by Greyhound to Point Pleasant, West Virginia, to pick up their station wagon at the Bryants'. Then, perhaps they'll drive down and meet us in Hot Springs—if our option is picked up again. Penni thinks there's an excellent chance the Manhattan Models will be here at the Pines for another two to four weeks or until the club closes for the summer. Everyone seems to love us! Acts come and go, but we stay on, something like a band. We've been here ten weeks already.

This afternoon, Mr. Owens took Penni, Allene, and me out for a drive along the winding, scenic Russellville Highway. Saw lots of trees and streams all the way to the Crystal Quartz Mine. Mr. Owens, being a newspaperman, is always reading when he isn't writing (or fishing). He knows how the crystals were formed and how they're excavated, cleaned, cut, and used. It was like being on a guided tour.

When we got back to Hot Springs, Mr. Owens took us to his place for dinner. While our friend prepared all the food, Penni, Allene, and I sat on the backyard patio and enjoyed the cool breeze.

Mr. Owens didn't want us to help, but as it got darker, Penni offered to hold a flashlight so our chef could see while cooking on the barbecue. Enjoyed a delicious dinner of steak, baked potatoes, and salad—lots of salad. Everything really good and NO FISH (surprised us!). Because of mosquitos humming over us, we sat close to insect-repellent lamps while eating. Kind of a bother, but the bugs love these warm evenings too, I guess.

Manhattan Models in Gypsy costumes
in Hot Springs, Arkansas, 1955.

Chapter Ten

May 10, 1955

Red left yesterday and Peg wrote the Herods right away about her plans to quit the Manhattan Cocktail Revue so she can marry the man she loves. The Herods will be very sorry to lose her, I'm sure. Penni's in kind of a daze. She feels Peg should reconsider. After all, Peg and Red haven't been together that much and never under normal conditions around home with parents, friends, and all that. And Red hasn't a job or training for a job. Penni thinks the Herods will be very upset, mainly because they are so far away. If only Peg could hold off until they come back, but I don't think she will. She wants to go to California next month, get a job in Merced to be close to Red, and that's that. Well, the three of us hope she knows what she's doing.

Had a nice surprise earlier today. Penni got a phone call from a bandleader who's just arrived in Hot Springs. This fellow was thrilled to learn from the newspaper that the Manhattan Models were featured at the Pines Supper Club. His name is Kent Porter, but none of us know him. Curiosity got the best of Penni, so she drove down to the Southern Grill where the Kent Porter Band had just opened. When she walked in the door, Penni told us later, the group started playing Burke and Johnston's "Pennies from Heaven." Turned out that Kent is the piano player we worked with last year at the Paramount Club in Albany, Georgia. He was playing with another band at the time and said he loved the Manhattan Cocktail Revue with its "variety package of fast-moving entertainment." Since getting his own group, he's been plugging our show everywhere he goes. That's what I call a valuable fan!

Our Chicago agent phoned Penni to confirm the revue's contract to begin county fairs on July 3. Allene and I would sure like to go home before then, but Penni feels we need to work as much as possible to save money. She's the boss. Penni's probably afraid she won't have enough to pay the Herods' bills for them while they're away. Today, for a treat, our leader went to the market and bought two pounds of rhubarb. She cooked it all up and, because Allene, Peg, and I weren't interested, ate the whole works herself. I'd say she kind of likes the stuff.Since he's leaving for Las Vegas on Saturday to take on a new job, Mr. Stanger was honored with a big going-away party at the Pines tonight. Mrs. Stanger was there, of course, with her little white poodle. This time they were both decked out in gold bows and baubles. Enjoyed a wonderful buffet dinner topped off with a large, special cake for dessert. "Good Luck" was scrawled in gold across the top of the white cake, above a pair of dice and horseshoes in frosting decoration. Naturally, champagne flowed freely.

The golf tournament in Hot Springs started yesterday causing business at the club to really boom, better than when the horse races were running. Kalantan is still on the show and is very popular. She looks terrific and always performs well, not like some exotic dancers who may have beautiful figures, but often just stroll around looking bored.

Went to the ladies' room tonight between shows and managed to witness something unusual. A girl was in there sobbing her head off. Naturally, I thought something terrible had happened. Then, I overheard her say that she just got married and had come to Hot Springs for her honeymoon! The groom was waiting now so they could leave the club and go to the hotel, but this girl was so nervous she wouldn't budge. She cried and cried. When I left, some kind lady was holding her hand and giving her motherly advice. I think the bride probably had too much to drink.

It started storming late in the evening, raining really hard with continuous thunder and lightning. When we got back to the cabin, Allene and I moved our bed away from the window. Just in case.

May 15, 1955

Last night, Penni found out from Mr. Stanger that we have only one week left at the Pines Supper Club. Boy, what a shock! Don't know what happened. We close on May 21. Now Penni will have to call Ross and hope he can find us work on rather short notice.

To get our minds off the latest news, the four of us went to a place called the IQ Zoo. Saw a raccoon that plays basketball, a tightrope-walking chicken, a pig that puts wooden nickels into a bank, and a chicken that plays golf and sells postcards! Had a great time and didn't worry a bit about where the Manhattan Models go from here. But, while anxiety about our next booking was forgotten, so was the whereabouts of the key to the cabin. Unfortunately, the MacDonalds, our handy, close-by club owners, were not around to unlock the door for us, so Penni poked a hole in one of the cabin's window screens. That done, she fiddled around and pried the window open. Because I'm the smallest, I got the honor of crawling through to open the door from the inside. Cheeka barked furiously at me. None of us realized before today what a good watchdog she is!

The Plymouth has been sputtering lately, therefore Penni, looking ahead to some traveling soon, is having Denny, the sax player with Kent Porter, look at it. Since he used to own a garage, he knows how to fix cars. Denny tore the engine apart first thing, fixing whatever he could find to fix. So far, he plans to put in a new oil filter, fuel pump, and gasket, and then change the oil. That should certainly help. According to Denny, it's remarkable the car kept running as long as it did.

A telegram came this evening from the Herods, advising Penni to go ahead and start looking for Peg's replacement. Reading between the lines, our leader feels it's a reluctant decision, as if they believe Peg will change her mind. Also, they are not pleased she would thoughtlessly go ahead and leave Penni on the spot, needing another dancer. The Herods' telegram came at about the same time Peg handed Penni a written resignation. She wants to be free two weeks from now to do as she pleases! This isn't like our close friend and fellow Manhattan Model of several years. She is infuriatingly calm and determined to leave us one girl short as far as getting jobs. I think Peg ought to know better, considering how her dancers deserted her two years ago. But her mind is made up. Penni, Allene, and I agree that she is rushing into something uncertain and may be sorry, and we told her as much. In response, Peg only blinked blue eyes at us.

Tonight, Cliff, Brenda, and the four of us did a special show downtown at the Elks to honor the mayor of Hot Springs. Had to squeeze this performance in between our regular shows at the Pines. The dressing room arrangement was a nightmare: changing outside in some storeroom, then maneuvering through the busy kitchen to the main hall, followed by a sprint across the dance floor to the bandstand, capped by a quick turnaround to face the audience! The crowd was wonderful, though. Just because they wanted to work with us, Kent Porter's Band was our accompaniment—and they were sure funny. Before we went on, the group stomped around the dance floor playing "When the Saints Go Marching In." Then, crazy Denny danced on and over the piano blowing his sax! These guys definitely want to do more than sit around on a bandstand.

I think Kent has a crush on Penni. He launched into "Pennies from Heaven" again when he saw her. It made her laugh, and that's good in view of the latest upsetting events. Penni says that Kent, as young as he is, has already suffered a heart attack. He laughs off the ticker problems, saying it's "more dignified than cancer." We all love him.

Allene and I, billed as the Halliday Twins, are doing our song and dance act at the club this week, and it's been going over great. We wear our new white silver-bugle-bead snowflake-decorated costumes, which truly look terrific under the lights. (Worth every pound of sweat we put into the sewing!) We're singing three songs ending with two choruses of tap dance after we pull off our skirts to show the leotards loaded with solid bugle-bead fringe. Sensational and nothing short of! Getting lots of oohs and aahs and whistles. Many people ask us why we haven't been doing our act all along as part of the show, and why, oh why, did we wait until our closing week? Oh well, not our decision, folks.

May 21, 1955

Ross called Penni last night to tell her the Manhattan Models go to Atlanta from here for a two-week engagement, so we got busy packing. This morning, our leader sent most of the costumes ahead by Railway Express to be sure they'd have plenty of time to reach Atlanta before our opening. Right after that, another call came from the agent informing her the job may have fallen through because the club is having financial trouble and is likely to close its doors at any time! Wonderful. Ross said he'd call Penni tonight to clue her in as to what's happening.

Wouldn't you know it? Peg hasn't wasted a minute. She's already made up her mind to go to California all the sooner if we don't get Atlanta. It seems a 24-hour notice is good enough when you're not working. Poor Penni. She's chewed her fingernails down to the nub and hasn't much to say to any of us, especially Peg. Our lovesick deserter got on the phone right away, trying to reach Red, hoping he'll come and get her as soon as possible.

This is our closing night, and friends at the club gave us funny parting gifts. Allene got a stuffed monkey, and I got some fudge in a toy dump truck. The four of us had some presents to give too. We appreciate the nice people we've met at the Pines and will miss the dealers, waiters, waitresses, band members, club owners, and our little maid who cleans the cabin. It's been a great three months. Mr. Owens came to bid us farewell and good luck but seemed to have trouble finding the words. I truly believe he will miss his "dancin' girls." We said goodbye to everyone.

Ross Russell did not call. We are now out of work.

May 22, 1955

Peg has gone to California. Yesterday, the three of us helped Miss Desperate and Determined to pack, then took her out for dinner to soothe hurt feelings and part as friends. It was pleasant. Peg absolutely bubbled over with excitement, chattering away about marrying Red and beginning a new life. She had no qualms whatsoever concerning dumping show business and the revue. This morning, Penni drove Peg to the bus depot and, of course, Allene and I went along. We put our friend on the westbound bus, carrying a makeup kit in one hand and a birdcage in the other. As she watched Peg waving goodbye out the window of the departing Greyhound, Penni got an idea. Her old buddy was not getting away that easily. The three of us jumped back into the Plymouth and followed the bus down the highway for about ten miles. Each time Penni passed the Greyhound and tooted the horn, Peg laughed and made faces at us out the window. Pretty soon we just fell back and turned around. Enough.

I feel sorry for Penni. She and Peg have been close for many years, not just in the revue, but when they were teenagers at Margaret Tapping's dance studio in Seattle. Over the years, the two shared the excitement of many, many performances. They've roomed together, double-dated together, confided in one another on all subjects—mainly the opposite sex, and even gotten silly drunk together. Penni and Peg wore matching outfits like sisters (sometimes) and mustard-seed friendship bracelets (always). Our leader will really miss her pal. Allene and I will too.

Back at the cabin things seemed gloomy so I decided to talk to Cheekaboom. I told her Peg and Billy were gone and not coming back. The little dog perked up her ears and cocked her head to one side like she was trying to understand what I said. Then, I tickled her tummy and she smiled, as she does sometimes, with her lips curled back, teeth and gums showing, and just wiggling all over. What a funny dog.

Haven't heard anything from Ross yet as to where we go next. No news is good news? Penni, Allene, and I seem adrift in space with nowhere to land. There's little conversation and nothing to laugh or smile about. Can't find the humor in our predicament, I guess, considering each of us is concerned about how long our money will last without another contract. The three of us will be harder to book now because we're not really a line of girls. Four is the minimum so Penni *must* find another dancer.

Lots of rain and clouds today. It cleared somewhat in the afternoon, so Allene decided we needed a refreshing, invigorating walk down our favorite road to lift our spirits. Bad idea! Ten minutes out, it started pouring down rain and wouldn't stop. We turned around and started running but got good and soaked in no time. Just then a car drove by, slammed on the brakes, and backed up. It was Kalantan. Someone we knew! She was more than happy to give us a lift back to the Pines and our cabin and didn't seem to care that we got her backseat wet. Nice person. The exotic dancer told us—and it certainly brightened our day—that our act looked really good, and she thought we should get bookings on our own. Best of all, she said we'd be surefire in Las Vegas. Allene laughed and said, "Don't tell Penni that."

Wanted to see the new show tonight, but it would have seemed funny to sit in the audience, so none of us bothered. We'd said goodbye to everyone, anyway, and couldn't do it all over again with nothing new to report regarding bookings. Felt down and dismal all evening. With the Herods, we always had somewhere to go.

Allene isn't talking much. I know she's thinking about what Kalantan said. I am too. What a neat break to get booked doing our act in Las Vegas! The Halliday Twins have enough material for two spots in two shows a night, using different numbers and different costumes. No problem there. What we don't have are recent photos or complete musical arrangements, but I would think a person could buy both in Las Vegas after getting a job and staying awhile. Kalantan says we're perfect for piano-bar entertainment, which uses small combos in a cozy nightclub atmosphere. Because she's worked the Last Frontier many times, Kalantan could probably get us booked there. I'm sure she'll help us.

May 25, 1955

We've been so thrilled with the idea of finally getting out on our own that Allene and I couldn't even sleep the night before last. Stayed up talking about it with Penni and eating a bunch of raisins. Since she hadn't heard from Ross, our leader was down in the dumps. She's thinking about driving home to Seattle, so could drop us off in Las Vegas, if that's where we want to go. How we each wish the Herods would call!

Anyway, couldn't eat anything all day yesterday because of a stomachache (too many raisins). Then, last night, Allene called home concerning leaving the Manhattan Models and going to Las Vegas. My sister told Mom that Penni can understand our wanting to quit and do our own act, so it wouldn't really be like deserting her. Suddenly an opportunity has fallen into our laps, Allene went on, and we're free (just like Peg) to do as we please. Well, Mom was sorry to hear we might leave the Manhattan Models, but thought working in Las Vegas was a wonderful chance we should take advantage of. If the two of us need money, she and Papa will send what they've saved to finish the house. Allene told Mom she'd let her know.

It's a risky plan, Allene thinks. What if we take money from Mom and Papa and can't pay them back? While on the phone, it occurred to my sister that we may get only a couple of weeks in Vegas and scramble for jobs after that. Better not chance it. Too bad we're not millionaires or at least a bit more self-confident. Felt depressed until Ross called Penni this morning. Finally, we have a job! The agent said the three of us can start work Monday, May 30, at the Gypsy Room in Atlanta for two weeks with options. Ross said it's the same club we worked two years ago—only it was called Mame's Latin Quarter then.

Jat got two of his songs recorded that summer: "My Mama Said" and "I'm in Love with Someone." There was an all-night radio show broadcasting across the street from Mame's, so our boss got interviewed once or twice and was able to plug those recordings, plus a couple of his other songs. The disc jockey was Bill George, and he interviewed each of us eventually. Good publicity for the Manhattan Cocktail Revue.

Ah, memories, but back to the present and current concerns! Drove into Hot Springs this morning and put in a change of address to General Delivery in Atlanta, Georgia. Picked up the mail. Allene heard from Dick, and Penni got a postcard from Peg, mailed somewhere in Texas. At least she's thinking of her old dancing buddies.

Because she never goes outside, Cheekaboom had to go to the vet to get her nails trimmed; Penni took care of that necessity while we were in town. Although, according to Penni, she was good at the doctor's, Cheeka must have been very frightened and shaken by the whole ordeal. Back at the cabin afterward, the little Chihuahua acted strange, eyeing each of us suspiciously, then hiding under a bed when anyone came near. Only a piece of steak got her out!

Have tried to get some packing done because we'll have to leave in the next few days. It is really quite warm—too hot for sunbathing or packing—but, although the days are scorchers, the evenings here are pleasantly balmy and still. We listen all night to the whip-poor-wills that must be sitting in nearby treetops, guaranteeing their warbling will be distinctly heard all around. Also, I like to watch the fireflies, flashing on and off like matches lit up then, *poof*, blown out. Fascinating critters. I will miss this place.

May 27, 1955

Last night, the three of us went to the Smorgasbord restaurant with Kent and the boys for our going away dinner. Had barbecued chicken, broiled fish, ravioli, and umpteen kinds of salad. Kent paid for our dinners. He's so great. I know if he had his way, he would make his group our personal band and travel everywhere with us. Anyhow, he wants us (especially Penni) to write him. Topping off the evening, our leader presented Kent with an ice cream cake for his birthday. It really isn't his big day yet, but we won't be here when it is. Anyway, Kent was totally surprised and delighted.

By the time we left the restaurant, a storm was in full swing with torrents of rain, crashing thunder, and dazzling lightning. All of us had to agree that Hot Springs has some really spectacular storms. Said goodbye quickly!

The turbulence seemed to get worse by the minute, and Penni, not able to see very well, drove slowly out to the Pines. Low spots in the road were thoroughly flooded, and the old Plymouth plowed and lurched through the water, stalling often. I thought we'd begin floating anytime! Even though it was pretty dark, I could see muddy water, laden with pieces of trees, bushes, boxes, bottles, and you name it, hitting the car broadside. It seemed an eternity before we finally reached the Pines Supper Club, hardly a place of refuge considering it resembled an island fortress being attacked by a roaring river!

Penni saw we couldn't drive up to our cabin. The water was too deep—up to the doorstep and maybe over—so she kept on driving down the submerged road until she found higher ground to park the car. We then took off our shoes and waded back toward the Pines and our soggy little cabin. Got thoroughly drenched, of course.

This morning there were crews of volunteers, old and young, male and female, out clearing the clutter from the road in front of the Pines, because once it quit raining, the water ran off quickly and left heaps of debris behind. Heard on the radio that a tornado hit fifteen miles up the highway from us. I believe it.

Later, Penni got a call from the Herods in London telling her she must hire someone soon. The full revue opens in Wichita, Kansas, on June 24 for a week's engagement at the Esquire Lounge. Peg called too. She has arrived in Merced and is happy.

Our original plan was to leave today for Atlanta. However, when Kent called to tell Penni goodbye, she mentioned the horrible drive home from the restaurant. Now Kent wants Denny to come over to check the Plymouth before we go anywhere. Guess all the water could have damaged something. Might be better to stay another night.

Chapter Eleven

May 31, 1955

Left Hot Springs two days ago and began the warm, long drive to Atlanta. Ate fruit for lunch in the car so we could make good time, but couldn't resist stopping in Tuscaloosa, Alabama, for ice cream. Tastes so good on a hot day! Drove on to Birmingham and pulled into a Howard Johnson's restaurant for dinner.

When we played Birmingham a couple of years ago, the temps were as high as now, so trying to go anywhere or do anything took determination. Mostly Allene and I walked, but the tar used to mend cracks in streets and sidewalks melted in the terrible heat and stuck on our shoes. Impossible to get off. One day, though, Peg, JoAleene, Allene, and I took a bus out to a nice park and braved the awful heat as we climbed 158 steps up to the foot of the big *Vulcan* statue, just to see the panoramic view of the city.

While in Birmingham, all of us in the revue lived right downtown at the Ranch House Motel and truly appreciated their air conditioning. In fact, Allene and I spent a great deal of time in our motel room sewing new cocktail dresses for ourselves or taking diction lessons from Betty, who always gave us things to do to improve our act. Also, it was a time of sewing wardrobe and rehearsing new dancers in an effort to launch Peg's ill-fated line.

With our minds still in the past, Penni drove over to Birmingham's

Lotus Club for a look at the place the revue played back then. It was a terrific spot to work, I remember, with a great band, rollout stage, and exceptional lights of all kinds and colors. The manager booked headliners like Janis Paige, Mel Tormé, the Harmonicats, Jan Garber, and Elmo Tanner. The building looks closed now.

Endured a nerve-wracking drive from Birmingham to Atlanta, thanks to the Plymouth's developing brake problems. Arrived in Atlanta in the cool of the evening and found a nice-looking place to stay called the Cherokee Rose Motel, located north of town. Since we feel we'd better keep trying to save money, the three of us checked into a spacious room with a kitchen. After putting our bags in the room, we all went out to eat. Found a Pig 'n Whistle not too far away that had good food.

Back from the restaurant, Penni, Allene, and I pushed furniture aside in our motel room to work out changes in our routines, going from a square to a triangle formation now that we are only three dancers. Slow going. Took hours and we were already pooped from the trip to begin with. But, worn out or not, we figured time had run out, and the positioning job had to be done. After all, we the Manhattan Models were opening the next day. Wrong!

In the morning, Penni called Ross to let him know we'd arrived, and got the bad news. Found out our opening at the Gypsy Room was not on May 30, as we had been told. It's been pushed back a week. No reason was given. Now we have another layover. Since the agent doesn't even have a club date lined up for us, Penni is upset and chewing her fingernails, like when Peg quit, because she's got bills to pay. Ross did say, however, that there is a good dancer from Atlanta who needs a job right away; Penni made arrangements to meet her tomorrow.

Went out for groceries and found an A&P not too far away. The three of us bought some cheap, economical provisions for the week ahead. Considering the day's disappointing news, no one felt much like fixing dinner, so Penni put together some grilled cheese sandwiches. However, since Cheeka didn't care for any part of such a skimpy dinner, Penni fixed her a boiled egg with buttered toast. It may be a while before she gets steak again! Then, while our leader went to a movie by herself, Allene and I sat at home and watched television. We have a set that plays forty-five minutes for a quarter, and if we fiddle with the antenna on top, we can get two channels. Spent a dollar but saw some good variety shows with Jack Benny and Bob Hope. Except for commercials, the shows seem to be set up like our revue with dancers to open the show, an act or two, skits and jokes, a "star," and then a closing production number. Looks drab, though, with no color.

June 3, 1955

Weather is chilly, and no one is very happy here in Atlanta. More than ever we're anxious for the Herods to come back. Have been rehearsing revised dance routines, going to movies, and watching Tennessee Ernie Ford on television every day. He calls himself the "pea picker" and has such a great time ad-libbing with his crew and the audience that he perks us up. Well, with no job the days are long, and there just isn't much else to do but sit around.

The last time we worked Atlanta, the whole revue stayed at the Imperial Hotel, right in town and very handy to everything. We used to practice our dances downstairs in the hotel's lounge called the Copa Caprice, a cozy little place with a nice floor where the manager didn't mind our coming in almost every day. The Manhattan Cocktail Revue was never booked at the Copa, as the club policy was to use mostly strippers or exotic dancers. I saw my first tassel twirler at the Imperial's Copa Caprice. She was a chunky brunette wearing a red fringe G-string to cover her crotch and red tassels to cover her nipples, which she whirled around to the right or to the left. Fantastic! I've never figured out how she did that. Her act reminded me of the time I saw Trudeen the "Quiver Queen" and how spellbound I was with her ability, not in tassel twirling, but shimmying, moving one row of the fringe on her costume at a time. Have to appreciate the time and energy these gals devote to their art.

Back then, Allene and I used to eat at Leb's or Cross Keys a lot, but one time, the whole revue went miles out of town to Aunt Fanny's Cabin, a restaurant within a really old building from Civil War days that had a big stone fireplace and great food. Ordered my favorite meal of steak and baked potato, but ran into trouble when I pulled off the parchment covering the potato to eat the skin. One bite and my teeth stuck together! Had a heck of a time trying to eat anything after that. Learned later that the raw potatoes are baked in hot rosin and then wrapped in parchment paper. People are *not* supposed to eat the skin. Bad idea, I think. After all, the skin's the best part of the potato.

Returning to problems here and now, I should report that the dancer Ross suggested for our line has already found a job. Fortunately, Penni had sent out a distress call earlier to Margaret Tapping, her former dance teacher in Seattle, asking for possible recruits to join the Manhattan Models. Luckily, Margaret found someone. Her name is Lois, and she goes to the University of Washington. Lois and Penni know each other from dance recital days. Our new girl arrives in Atlanta next week, and she's so anxious to join the Manhattan Models, Penni said, her bags are already packed!

Lois and our leader probably have a lot in common since Penni went to the University of Washington too, off and on. Her parents in Seattle always wanted their daughter to get serious about continuing her education. That meant forgetting show business and traveling around so she could return to college. Penni almost did, too. The last time we played Atlanta, she was forced to give it some serious thought. Her folks promised to buy her a convertible car if she'd come back home and finish college. Penni became gloomy for a while as she tried to make up her mind. Fortunately, she decided that the convertible and college could wait.

Got a letter from the Herods with news about what they did when Jat finished his theater tour in Great Britain. It seems they sailed to the continent by way of Hook of Holland, then took a train to Paris and stayed in a little hotel in Montmartre. Betty wrote that the three of them had a wonderful time playing tourist and seeing popular attractions like the Louvre, Eiffel Tower, Palace of Versailles, and Notre-Dame. Plus, eating, eating, eating. I guess they walked up and down the Champs-Élysées and sat at the sidewalk cafés watching people too. By now they must be back in London getting ready to catch the train to Portsmouth where they'll board the French ocean liner for New York.

Today, because of the brake trouble we had getting here, Penni has taken the old Plymouth in for more repairs. She figures she'll need to buy new brakes. It's too bad Denny isn't here in Atlanta. How great it was in Hot Springs to have someone around who knew something about cars and how everything operates. He only charged for what needed replacing too. No labor costs.

Since she hadn't heard from Dick in a couple of weeks, Allene was jubilant when she received a letter from him. He is still in Jackson Hole, but unfortunately, his friend Dave took off, leaving Dick to manage the hot dog stand by himself. Because it's the tourist season, business is probably booming, and my sister's favorite man must be very busy. Dick reports he still loves Jackson Hole, with its nearby mountains and lakes, and doesn't ever want to go back to Los Angeles. That being the case, the three of us sure hope he can make a go of his hot dog stand. I think he'll need to hire someone to help him, though.

My sister baked some cookies today to send to the Kent Porter Band in Hot Springs, all the time thinking of Dick, I'll bet, since after that she baked another batch to send to him.

June 5, 1955

Yesterday, the three of us went over to the Gypsy Room, the club we'll be working, to check it out. Discovered the club's stage is smaller now than when the place was called Mame's Latin Quarter. We're expected to perform within an area of about ten feet by ten feet, which is pretty small for three dancers. So, besides concentrating on our modified dance routines, we have the challenge of limited space. When she got back to our motel room, Penni marked off a ten-by-ten square, and we right away began practicing dancing extra close together. Had to laugh. Did several routines in our new, tighter triangle formation, and our leader fell off her "stage" six times!

This morning, Penni tried to eat an egg for breakfast, but Cheekaboom, who loves eggs, bugged and bugged her. Poor Penni hardly got a bite and ended up giving most of her breakfast to the Chihuahua. Cheeka's such a little dog, but she can sure eat, especially eggs and steak. Sometimes, though, she gets too big a chunk of something and chokes on it. The only thing to do then is hold her upside down by her hind legs and thump her on the back until the piece falls out of her mouth. I saw Betty do that once.

Cloudy, blowy, cool weather today. So much for the "Sunny South." Allene and I watched Tennessee Ernie Ford, then went for a walk to see if we could find a library around here. No soap. Although we're in a nice section of Atlanta, there doesn't seem to be much to do. I could sit in the room and sew beads—an endless task—but I'm tired of just sitting around. I Guess Allene is too. Ditto for Penni. She's gone somewhere just to get away from the walls! We dare not go shopping or to a restaurant until we're sure we've got a job.

June 8, 1955

Began at the Gypsy Room two nights ago, doing a couple of shows a night, opening and closing each performance, like at the Pines Supper Club. In the first show, the three of us do the Charleston and Gypsy, and in the second, it's the Samba and Football routines. We are so crowded we hardly dance at all, just kind of shuffle around, changing places carefully, especially when doing turns.

Our emcee is Bobby Baxter, a small, handsome but worried-looking man who wears a toupee. (I'll bet his hair fell out from stress!) Allene and I like him, though he seems restless, has to move, has to check this or that, and make sure everything's okay. I hope he doesn't have ulcers, but he certainly looks like he's in pain most of the time.

Bobby called us back after the Charleston on opening night and asked if we could do something extra. (You bet!) After talking to the band leader, my sister and I felt brave enough to break in a new tap dance Betty showed us last year. The music is Fats Waller's "Honeysuckle Rose" and, thank goodness, this band knew it and could play two choruses for us, because we sure don't have any written arrangements yet. Things went amazingly well considering how impromptu the request was, and the Halliday Twins got great applause. Although small, the stage has a wonderful floor for tapping, so we sounded good, even without taps on our shoes. Very encouraging!

With us on the show is Dariece, a tall, blonde, gorgeous exotic dancer, with a kind of wide-eyed, innocent look about her. One number she does is Little Bo-Peep with the accent on "peep" as she wears a see-through hoop skirt topped by perky rosebud pasties on her large breasts. I wouldn't say she dances. She just walks and turns slowly like a painted figurine on a music box.

I believe Dariece may not be able to see very well, and that's why her eyes are always so wide open. After the show last night, Bobby, Dariece, and the three of us went to breakfast with our friends, some Venezuelan engineers we met at the club. Dariece ordered two fried eggs and toast. When her breakfast arrived, she complained to the waitress that she ordered two not three fried eggs. We all stared at her. She couldn't see that the third "egg" was white hominy grits with melted butter in the center. Wow.

Ross came to the club tonight, arriving late, just as we were getting ready for the first show, and leaving early before any of us could dress and get out front to see him. Ominous! We presume he *did* catch the first show. Penni had hoped to talk to him about the Herods' return and to let him know that she'd hired a dancer.

June 11, 1955

Yesterday, the three of us went to the airport to meet Lois, who flew in from Seattle. Her flight was two hours late, so we waited around the terminal, watching planes coming and going until hers landed. All in all, the trip from Seattle to Atlanta took sixteen hours! When the passengers finally disembarked, Penni spotted Lois right away. Our new girl stepped off the plane looking a bit frazzled and dazed, but when Lois entered the terminal and saw Penni, she flashed a big smile. Like our leader, Lois is a redhead, born and raised in Seattle. She seems very nice. Driving back to the Cherokee Rose, we kicked around ideas for a stage name, because Lois doesn't seem quite right. Lois laughed, saying she didn't care what she was called as long as it wasn't Rusty. We all agreed that Lori sounded better, so that's her new name.

Allene fixed cube steaks for everyone after we got our new girl moved in. Then, it was time for Penni, Allene, and I to get ready for work. We thought Lori would want to rest after the long, dragged-out flight, but no, Lori was anxious to see the show. Coming with us to the Gypsy Room, our new dancer thoroughly enjoyed both performances. Then, to add to Lori's first day in Atlanta, the four of us rushed over to Joe Cotton's steak room between our shows, to see The Crew-Cuts, a Canadian recording group who had a hit record a few years back. They were great, and Lori seemed absolutely thrilled to learn they are our competition!

Today, Penni began rehearsing with Lori. Apparently, the newest recruit does some ballet and tap but is foremost an acrobatic dancer. In any case, the two of them are trying to maneuver in our motel room, which is not very big for learning dance routines. Lori is having some trouble picking up the number. Our routines are not difficult, but we do move around a lot. Allene and I will get pulled into these rehearsals soon because of the lineup and placement. These are important considerations when working with other people, and what makes the difference between dancers looking good or bad. Just as necessary as learning the steps, really. I would say the moving group is more important than the individual dancer. (Pat, you are so smart sometimes.) I think Lori just needs to relax and find the rhythm. She seems so intent on which step comes next that she rushes the beat. I remember that Allene and I had rhythm problems when we first joined the revue. Betty said both of us anticipated the steps and weren't listening to the music, so she ordered us to practice keeping time with whatever song the band played between shows, tapping the beat on the table. I think it helped. Lori may need to do that too.

Got a letter from Mom today. She said Papa's upset and has been pacing the floor. They just received the booklet advertising Atlanta nightlife that Allene sent to them in Anacortes. Right away, Papa glanced through it and saw the ad for the Gypsy Room, which showed a picture of Dariece, nearly naked in a flimsy gown. Of course, the Manhattan Models are mentioned in the ad too, but with no photo. Anyway, according to Mom, Papa took one look at busty, hippy Dariece in her see-through negligee and thought it was yours truly. Now, he wants Allene and me to come home on the double. What a laugh! The only thing I have in common with Dariece is blonde hair.

Mom went on to say she told Papa she was certain I would never parade around with nothing on and was quite sure the picture was not of "little Pat." But he still isn't convinced, she wrote. Tonight, worried about the trouble she'd caused, Allene called home before we went to the club. Papa had calmed down concerning the photo but thought we should come home soon to see the house and all the progress. That sure would be nice, but we can't. In the meantime, I guess, Allene won't send them any more nightlife booklets.

June 20, 1955

Closed the Gypsy Room two nights ago. To make the most of a good situation, Allene and I decided to break in our Latin dance while we had an excellent band and an emcee who constantly encouraged us to do more. Penni said she didn't care. Besides, it was our last night. Having finished the costumes and practiced the dance routine all afternoon, Allene and I felt ready. Talked over the music with the band, then, right after the opening number, changed quickly into our black and white polka-dot bikini costumes with the red-orange bustles in the back and the black boa trim in the front. It was so funny. Dariece, with her poor eyesight, stared at the black fluff on the front of our bikinis and remarked that she thought we were natural blondes! The dance went fine, but I think my sister wants to redo the front of the costume.

Since his incoming act can't make the Monday opening date, Ross had asked Penni if the line could stay over one more day. Penni said no. I believe she's still peeved at him, feeling he could have helped us more. Actually, I think getting another day's pay whenever possible is always a good idea, but nobody asked me.

Anyway, Penni wants Monday off. Then, she can take her time driving to Wichita, our next job. Kent and the band are working Shreveport now, so I'm sure she'll point the Plymouth in that direction. I'd bet money our leader really goes for that crazy piano player. Well, Kent's a nut but a dear one, and Wichita's about 900 miles from here, so we'll have to stop somewhere. Penni's already shipped the costumes and music to Kansas by Railway Express.

The Herods should be arriving in New York any time now. They'll have to pick up the station wagon in Point Pleasant and then drive over to Wichita. Don't know when the three of them or the four of us will arrive in Wichita, as it's a totally new and unfamiliar destination. All we know is that the Manhattan Cocktail Revue is booked for one week at a place called the Esquire Lounge. It will be good to see our bosses and JoAleene again.

Late yesterday, we left Atlanta and drove down to Albany, stopping for something to eat at Stem's, our favorite 24-hour café. The waitresses remembered us and asked about Peg. Guess the Club Paramount has new owners again. From Albany, we traveled all night, stopping in Mobile, Alabama, for breakfast. What a great place! Allene and I took Cheeka for a walk and to get some exercise ourselves. Personally, I'd liked to have stayed longer and seen more of that sunny city on the water, but we were just passing through. Penni, of course, was anxious to go on to New Orleans.

Continued along the coast and through Biloxi, a very special place for Allene and me. We felt nostalgic seeing the resort area with its tall palms and white beaches again. Biloxi was where we met the Herods, Peg, Joann, and Penni and broke in as dancers with the Manhattan Cocktail Revue at a club called The Stables. Allene and I lived in a motel next to the club, a handy arrangement—although we never had any hot water—allowing us to rehearse on the dance floor every day for hours. Afraid we might get shipped right back to Anacortes, Big Sister and I were determined to learn everything fast and get glamourous in a hurry! As I recall, we bought chignons so we could wear our long hair swept high in a bun to appear older and sophisticated. We lied that we were twenty-one and twenty-two. The Herods said nothing, but I know we didn't fool them. In any case, they liked us, turned us into twins, and never sent us back home.

Took a long, sentimental look at the old Stables Club as we drove by. It doesn't appear to be a night spot anymore, just a café.

Our next stop was New Orleans. Penni pulled in and parked at the Tulane Motel, a decent-looking place on the outskirts of the city, then went into the office for information while the rest of us waited in the car. Cheekaboom was in the front seat on Lori's lap, gazing out the closed window, when suddenly the fur on her back bristled, and she began to growl. We saw that a very large, brown fuzzy dog was approaching the car! Cheeka hopped back and forth snapping and snarling through the pane at that huge dog—until Lori lowered the car window to shoo the big guy away. Cheekaboom then shut right up and scooted under the steering wheel to hide. Smart little dog.

After checking into the motel, we took naps before getting cleaned up to go to dinner. We'd heard of a terrific French restaurant located in the old slave market part of New Orleans. Expecting an establishment like Antoine's, the four of us wore our nicest cocktail dresses, jewelry, and fur stoles. What a shock when we saw that the fancy restaurant was instead a place with sawdust on the floors, bright lights, lots of smoke, and noisy diners! Found an empty table and sat down just as a waiter reached over us to slap four hunks of French bread on its bare wooden surface. Hurrying back and forth, our waiter soon returned with a huge tureen of steaming vegetable soup to kick off the meal. The four of us were a little surprised with all the service and food since we hadn't even seen a menu! Several wonderful courses followed: baked fish, ham with melted cheese, small broiled steaks with little tomatoes, asparagus, and watercress salad. Dessert was a chocolate-cream something or other we were too full to eat. The waiter insisted, so we had him bring one dessert and four spoons. All in all, we were served an unforgettable and sensational dinner that was not expensive.

Today, we walked around New Orleans, peeking into colorful courtyards and admiring the old buildings with their lacy balconies. Lots of picturesque little side streets and alleyways too. This city is quite unique, not at all like other cities we've been to in the country. Kind of a reminder that the French came through here first and set the style for buildings and streets. Watched the praline-making process at Kate Latterer's shop and bought several boxes of the very sweet pecan candy patties. Can't eat many of them, though. Pure sugar.

June 23, 1955

Yesterday, after Penni repacked the Plymouth to get all the souvenirs in, we left New Orleans and drove up to Shreveport, arriving in the late afternoon. Allene and I haven't been in Shreveport since 1953, when the revue performed at the Stork Club in nearby Bossier City. Stopped for some fruit at the Jitney Jungle, then checked into the Kickapoo Courts, the rambling ranch-style motel we lived in before while working this engagement.

Don't especially remember the booking, except for one evening between shows when my dress zipper split wide open while I sat on a stool at the bar sipping a Grasshopper. Other than that, we spent the best Hallowe'en ever! Early in the evening, before going to the club, Penni, Peg, Allene, and I took JoAleene trick-or-treating because the Herods' daughter had never done that before. She got all excited, and her eyes were enormous as she watched other costumed kids with jack-o'-lanterns running from house to house. Had a great time and gave JoAleene most of the loot—enough candy to last her a year.

Kent Porter's band is currently playing at the Stork Club. Originally, Kent wanted the Manhattan Models to play the date with him, but sometimes things just don't work out. At the time, Penni thought we'd still be booked at the Pines in Hot Springs, so couldn't sign another contract. Would have been fun to perform here with them.

Went to dinner at the club and to hear Kent's group. Not much of a crowd or a show—just an emcee and a stripper. The emcee-comic was a little guy, kind of expressionless, who wore a yellow fright wig, told knock-knock jokes, and looked like he wished he were somewhere else. He didn't go over well. I think he knew he was "dying" but kept on with his routine. If no one else laughed, he did.

The stripper was an old gal strutting around trying to look alluring. I don't believe anyone really wanted to see her drop off her gauzy, something-like-sheer-curtain gown. Our good friend Kent seemed exceptionally happy to see Penni again, and it appears she's made another conquest for her long boyfriend list. Also, I noticed Denny, the saxophone-playing auto mechanic, being very attentive to my sister, hardly taking his eyes off her. (It's that smile of hers.)

This morning, we left Shreveport and drove into Texas. Our first stop was Mt. Pleasant where Allene and I bought some fruit at a Safeway. Because the weather's so sizzling hot, we're only interested in eating things cold and juicy. I don't know how they could, but Penni and Lori went to a café and downed a hot meal of cheeseburgers and French fries.

On to Norman, Oklahoma—a memorable place for its location within the bleak, parched, super-hot territory. Stopped at the Gilt Dairy and indulged in large cups of ice cream because we were all dying of the heat. It certainly hit the spot. Even Cheeka had some. Driving was straight and easy, so Penni wanted to keep on despite the high temps and desolate region.

Rolled into Wichita, Kansas in the early evening (still darn warm), had a pretty good dinner at the Continental Grill, then checked into the Anchor Motel for the night. Of course, we don't know where the Esquire Lounge is from here or if the Herods have arrived. The plan is to make some phone calls and get directions tomorrow sometime before band rehearsal.

Kent Porter at the piano and Denny (at far right) on the bandstand with saxophone.

Halliday Twins – Pat and Allene – in white beaded song and dance speciality routine at Hilltop Casino in East Dubuque, Illinois, 1955.

Part Three

~

A Really Big Decision

*County Fair stage Manhattan Models take
a bow in Beach costumes, 1955.*

County Fairgrounds, 1955.

Chapter Twelve

June 25, 1955

Yesterday afternoon, we checked out of the Anchor Motel and went looking for the Esquire Lounge. Got directions from a mechanic at a Chevron station and found the club several miles out of Wichita on a golf course. The whole area resembles an oasis dropped in the midst of a dustbowl. Although small, the Esquire looked like a spanking new, glorified clubhouse surrounded by velvety golf links. Fortunately for us, close by was an equally new-looking Holiday Inn with a swimming pool full of sparkling blue water, impossible to resist after all the heat we'd been through. The motel's rather expensive, so the four of us rented one big room ($55 a week) to save money.

Walked over to the Esquire Lounge for news regarding our bosses and learned that the Herods left word they had arrived and are staying at a motel in town. We hurried back to our room where Penni gave them a call. Out they came right away to the Holiday Inn, laden with souvenirs for everyone: perfume, candy, menus, and programs. All smiles, they appeared really happy to be back.

While staying in Great Britain turned out to be a hardship concerning living and working conditions, Betty said, traveling over to the continent was pure joy and the highlight of the whole trip. I wasn't surprised to see that the three of them looked heavier since, according to Jat, they "ate their way through Paris."

JoAleene looks taller and somewhat gangly now. The familiar

little-girl dress she had on with the big collar and sash didn't seem to suit her anymore. And, poor thing, as soon as she saw Cheekaboom, the Herods' daughter rushed over to pick the little dog up only to have it snap and snarl then run under the bed! Surprised all of us and I think hurt JoAleene's feelings. In fact, the Chihuahua acted as though her owners were strangers until Betty opened a wardrobe case and tried on one of her costumes. Then, Cheeka got all excited, wagging her tail, wiggling all over, and laughing the way she does.

What's left of our red bangs simply fascinated Jat, who just kept staring at Allene and me. He said he'd never seen anything so peculiar and appeared a bit embarrassed to have been caught looking. Anyway, the Herods seem very pleased to see Penni, Allene, and me and to meet Lori. Nothing was said about Peg and Red. Episode closed, I guess.

Went back over to the Esquire for band rehearsal at two o'clock. The band boys are on the young side but very enthusiastic and cooperative. Good musicians too. They cut the show arrangements just fine. It was wonderful to have Jat doing the rehearsing again, as he knows so much more about the music than any of us dancers. Since it had been several months without the Herods, the Manhattan Models seriously needed complete run-throughs of each of our numbers, mainly to get used to performing with Betty again! Of course, for Lori, everything was new and different. I could tell she was concentrating really hard on getting everything right, considering the Herods would be watching how she looked and moved.

Afterward, while moving costumes and props, we found out there's a television set in our dressing room—just in case anyone finds they have nothing to do between numbers. Boy, that's really something.

It was an unusual (to say the least) opening night. Our first number for the dinner show was the Charleston, and Lori did just fine breaking in. At least, as far as I could tell, she was where she should be and didn't louse up any steps. But when Betty came onstage to begin her solo, she slipped and fell! There she was flat on her back, feet all tangled in her fringe costume, thrashing around on the floor like a fish in a net! Not knowing what else to do, the four of us danced around or stepped over her. Super.

Then, Betty began to laugh. Then, the audience began to laugh. Then, making the most of the moment, Jat winced and covered his eyes. He shook his head, then bent down and pulled his wife to her feet, while holding his back like he'd just yanked it out. More laughs. Following that rare opening to our show, Jat learned we had a celebrity in the audience. Tex Ritter, the well-known actor and singing cowboy was out front. With much coaxing and audience applause, our boss got him up to sing his big hit, "High Noon," written by Dimitri Tiomkin. (I love his name. It sounds so exotic.) Embarrassing moment! The musicians were totally surprised and apparently unprepared to handle something impromptu. It looked like amateur hour on the bandstand until Jat intervened by taking the lead, playing the melody on his violin while stomping his foot to help the drummer with the syncopated beat. Really saved the situation for everyone.

Too bad we are only staying one week. People here are so pleasant and easygoing at the Esquire. Because of the club, and the Holiday Inn with its wonderful pool just outside our room, all of us are enjoying Wichita. It's been more like a vacation than playing a job. Unfortunately, we close on June 30 and drive up to Minnesota for the totally new experience of doing county fairs.

June 27, 1955

JoAleene came out to use the swimming pool this morning and told us her grandparents, Captain Billy and Josie Bryant, will do the fairs too—not as part of the grandstand show but selling items in booths. That way they can travel around with us, living in a trailer, instead of staying home for the summer. Following the Bryants' lead, Jat and Betty plan to buy a trailer for camping like gypsies right on the fairgrounds too. I'm not sure I'd go for that. Too much togetherness.

Went to town for the mail and to send home our cocktail dresses and high heels. Since we'll probably be living in shorts, tee shirts, and pedal pushers on the fair circuit, it's a cinch we won't need nightclub attire. Also, Allene and I finally shipped our fur stoles to Dubuque for storage until fall.

Penni heard from JoAleene that our county fairs are located in or near teensy, tiny, small towns—mere pinpoints on a map. Now, she's worried there won't be any car repair garages, if the Plymouth acts up, or even gas stations for fill-ups. And something else occurred to me: what happens if there aren't any motels or hotels, either? Betty advised us to think positively, but I don't see how that can help.

Allene received some chocolates today from Don in Denver. They weren't smashed or melted or anything. Don wrote on the enclosed card that he really misses my sister and her beautiful smile and wishes the revue would get booked in Denver so he can see her again. I don't remember diligent, determined Don being all that attentive to Allene (or anybody else) when the revue played the Last Chance Saloon in Anchorage, where we met him originally. And I'm certain Allene never told him she loves chocolates, yet that idea seems set in Don's mind as a way to impress her. Sometimes I wonder if this fellow has a financial interest in Whitman's Sampler!

Big news! Penni just read her mail and announced that she got a letter from Peg saying that she and Red tied the knot at a little chapel in Reno a few days ago. Now they are back in Merced where Red will look for work. Seems to me, since the groom has no job training or skills, the bride better seek employment too. Someone has to pay the bills.

Betty called a rehearsal for this afternoon to clean up a bunch of things. And, boy, did we get chewed out! Our boss feels we've gotten sloppy and have been fudging on steps in the dance routines. We aren't together anymore, she says, or even lined up well. It's as though none of us ever bothers to glance over at the person next to her. Well, that figures. We haven't had a decent place to rehearse since the Pines Supper Club and, of course, we haven't had Betty around cracking the whip. Poor Lori. Betty corrected her repeatedly on the lineup and finally told her that, if she can't tell whether her positioning is good or bad, she should get her eyes checked. For sure, Lori's not used to dancing with a group, plus there's a lot to remember when you're new. I just hope she doesn't get discouraged.

Because the food is excellent here at the Holiday Inn, we eat in the coffee shop a lot. But, tonight, for a change, Penni, Lori, Allene, and I went to El Charro to dine, since the Herods recommended it.

We thoroughly enjoyed ourselves at this terrific Mexican restaurant, specializing in scrumptious enchiladas and rellenos, served up while dreamy recorded Latin-beat guitar music played. Heaven!

Found out how much we miss taking care of Cheekaboom. Although she is back with the Herods, Penni, Allene, and I saved some of our dinner for the dog. Cheeka might not care for Mexican food, but I'll bet she'll give it a try.

July 2, 1955

Had a combined birthday party for Lori and JoAleene on June 30, closing night at the Esquire. While it was our new girl's special day, we included JoAleene because she was in England on her birthday and the Manhattan Models couldn't celebrate with her. Took over a big table in the back of the club and piled it with gifts at one end for both honorees, while waiters tied pink balloons to the chairs for a festive look. Later, all of us enjoyed wonderful steak dinners for the occasion, then a huge ice cream cake in several flavors. Lori let JoAleene blow out the eleven candles.

Spent the next morning splashing around the pool one last time before having to check out and hit the road. The Herods came over and joined us. Seeing all of us together, the manager of the Holiday Inn stopped by and complimented us on our show. He said he wanted to treat everybody to anything we'd like from the motel coffee shop's soda fountain, and not necessarily what's on the regular menu. We could create something of our own by using ice cream flavor combinations, various toppings, nuts, chocolate chips, you name it!

So, after a lovely swim, everybody changed quickly and headed for the coffee shop, where each of us had a great time behind the counter helping ourselves to the fabulous assortment of good stuff! I fixed myself a small, loaded-up-with-goodies chocolate sundae (my favorite) and couldn't even finish it. Allene had plain butterscotch while JoAleene ate the most: a gargantuan banana split with six scoops of ice cream, drizzled with chocolate, caramel, and strawberry sauce, then topped with peanuts and whipped cream. Well, she can still afford the calories.

Following her ice cream lunch, Penni took the Plymouth in for a tune-up and radiator check. Then, in the late afternoon, when the heat was terrible, we rolled out of Wichita and headed north to farm country, the four of us truly wondering what the Herods had booked us into. We'd seen state fairs and their big, all-star shows but really couldn't imagine what a county fair could present for entertainment. Penni drove all night through flat, open countryside, making good time because there weren't many cars and trucks on the road. Not many towns, either. In fact, except for the two-lane highway, we saw few signs of civilization, just a light here and there, like maybe a distant farmhouse.

Sometime after midnight, feeling hungry and skeptical about spotting a café anywhere, the four of us kept an eye out for 24-hour truck stops—and luckily found one where three highways converge. It was called Stanley Corners, and, although nothing fancy, a welcome sight! I think I've never had such a delicious cheeseburger. The four of us were so hungry, we ate everything but the plates—and in record time, I'd say, judging by the look on our waiter's face. He was a cute guy and must have felt sorry for us since he brought extra cheese and buns, which we promptly devoured.

Arrived this morning in Fertile, Minnesota—population 938— and were we ever glad to see the city limits sign! The entire trip covered 800 miles of driving on back roads or narrow little highways. Thanks to someone connected with the fairs, Penni, Lori, Allene, and I are staying with a family called the Roes in a house about a half block from the fairgrounds. The four of us occupy two bedrooms and feel lucky to get them since there are no hotels in Fertile. It's going to be very pleasant and different to live in someone's home.

Unloaded the car, then went looking for the Herods at the fairgrounds. Saw some activity at several old exhibit buildings and barns in the middle of the flat field, then walked around, noting that a few trailers had pulled in. The Herods arrived pulling a small trailer to join the others.

Lots of people wrestled with ropes and canvas, attempting to raise tents, while a crew of roustabouts unloaded big trucks of equipment and carnival rides onto an open area.

Went back and got the Plymouth so we could drive through Fertile (which took about five seconds) for a look around. This is the tiniest town I've ever seen! Found one single, solitary place to eat called Louie's, so we went in to try their cheeseburgers. Not bad. Seems to be a family-run café with friendly people serving good food, but I can't imagine how they stay in business. Considering it is the Fourth of July weekend, this town's pretty dead. We might just as well be on another planet.

July 5, 1955

The Fertile County Fair opened at noon on July 3, and the Manhattan Cocktail Revue did a matinee for a small audience. We worked with Billy Pappin, a harmonica-playing emcee; a trained bear on a bicycle; a balloon act; and some aerialists. Unlike anything we've performed on before, our "stage" was a roofless, outdoor, wooden platform with painted plywood "wings" at either side, depicting country scenes of pastures, silos, cows, chickens, and all. Entertainers faced a covered grandstand on the other side of a racetrack that circled the stage, and our handy dressing room was in the back of a dark, hot, stuffy truck. I spent my first day dancing for county fairs with the sun in my eyes, wind through my hair, and dust up my nose. Wonderful.

After the show, Allene and I went in search of the Bryants to say hello, as we hadn't seen them since the Paramount Club in Albany. Found them happily setting up business within a row of other vendors. JoAleene was on hand to help stack packages of yarn and, more or less, to put items in place. The Bryants each have small, canvas-covered stands loaded with merchandise. Surrounded by her colorful displays, Josie plans to sell rugs and punchboard sets for making pillow or chair covers. Captain Billy, in the stand next to hers, will peddle fountain pens and has about a hundred spread over a table. Knowing him, he'll kid everyone who stops by or tell them a joke, whether they buy anything or not! Both Bryants are great talkers, so should do well selling just about anything they want to, although I believe they're here more for fun than profit.

Chatted a while, then Allene and I crossed the fairgrounds looking for somewhere to eat and ended up at the Lutheran Ladies

Aid Booth. Saw our landlady, Mrs. Roe, dishing up Swedish meatballs and homemade pies. Had to have some of those! Despite the adverse dining conditions of a stifling hot tent, flies, and crowded benches and tables, Allene and I agreed the dinner was absolutely delicious. Met friends of the Roes—Swensons and Jorgesons—also having dinner. (We seem to be in Scandinavian territory.)

Had to laugh. Penni and Lori drove over to Louie's for dinner, and both ordered sandwiches, they told us. After Lori had eaten about half of hers, she discovered she'd chewed into some paper. At first, she was shocked, then she started laughing and began to choke. The cook (a shy guy) came running to the rescue with a glass of water and an explanation. Since he was unable to get Lori's attention from the kitchen, he had sent a note in her sandwich, asking for a date.

The evening performance went slightly better than the matinee. That is, the band did a better job playing the music, and more people sat in the grandstand. Plus, temps were cooler, and the wind had died down. To tell the truth, it was a gloriously gorgeous summer evening. Waiting to go on, I couldn't help but notice the organ music and the swirling lights of the midway, with kids happily screaming away, having a big time. Perfect—except for all the mosquitoes buzzing around.

Last night, the Fourth, we worked with totally different acts on the show. Had a bell-ringing emcee, jugglers, a tightrope walker, and the Whiz Kids (unicyclists). The fairgrounds were really packed for the Independence Day celebration. People must come from miles around; they're sure not all from this tiny place.

Today is the last day of the county fair in Fertile. Because we don't have to do any shows, Allene and I decided to just enjoy ourselves, so went over to the fairgrounds and rode on the Ferris wheel. It wasn't very exciting, but going up high is a good way to see the surrounding countryside (farms in every direction), plus it didn't cost a thing. Found out we can ride on anything in the midway for nothing because we're now part of the fair "family." Pretty neat deal.

Walked from the midway over to the track to see the ostrich and camel races in front of the grandstand. To kick things off, there was a stunt rider like in the movies, jumping on and off a galloping horse, followed by a clown with an umbrella sitting backward on a donkey trying to make it move. The donkey wouldn't budge and kept flipping the clown off. Lots of laughs! The kids really love that crazy stuff. After that, a girl resembling an Arabian princess, with veils and all, rode an elephant, that was draped in a tasseled robe, onto the track, made a big circle to be sure everyone had a good look, then stopped. The "princess" slid down the elephant's trunk to the ground, where she took him through some tricks and poses. Good act, very impressive, and of course, a great hit. Following that, some fellow attempted to ride a zebra but got thrown off. Lots of variety at this fair, but we never found the ostriches and camels.

Went by the Herods' trailer on our way back home. Like the others, they're parked right on the fairgrounds near the grandstand and seem very happy living with no conveniences in a sixteen-foot teardrop trailer where everything is compact and handy. Betty said they can't stay inside except to sleep because it's too cozy and "hot as a furnace in winter" most of the time. To give them some overflow space, an awning-covered area with a picnic table is right outside their trailer door. And boy, do they need it! When Betty opened the trailer door to get something, like old-time radio's Fibber McGee's closet, all kinds of belongings tumbled out.

Seems to me trailers are strictly a fair-weather living arrangement and wouldn't suit everyone (like yours truly). The Herods are lucky the thunderstorms that come through every day have occurred only late at night when they're inside their little home. Actually, all of us are lucky no storms have hit during our open-air performances. Haven't heard from anyone so far, but Allene has written Kalantan, who is now back in Las Vegas, just to stay in touch. It's funny Betty hasn't asked us about the act or how the costumes are coming along. Could be she wants to relax for a while and enjoy this fair thing.

July 9, 1955

Left Fertile a couple of days ago. Just before we pulled out, the Roes invited us to sit on their front porch and enjoy angel food cake, cookies, and punch. A nice treat and a happy send-off. We had to wait until evening anyway so the drive would be cooler. It's not just for passenger comfort either. I think Penni's afraid the old Plymouth might boil over or blow a tire if she drove it during the daytime heat.

Took an hour and a half to go the one hundred miles to Barnesville, Minnesota, our next job, then hunted for a motel to live in, since the rented rooms in people's homes were already taken by the time we arrived. Checked into Hasse's, the only motel around. It's okay. Unfortunately, we have no drawers or closets in the room and must literally live out of suitcases. Then, because nothing in Barnesville looked inviting, the four of us piled back into the car to go another twenty-two miles to Fargo, North Dakota, for a decent dinner. So, right off the bat, none of the Manhattan Models were happy with Barnesville.

Fortunately, our surroundings appeared better the next day. Hasse's Motel is located about ten blocks from the fairgrounds, a wonderful discovery, as far as Allene's concerned. We can always use the exercise, she says. So, heat or no heat, while Penni and Lori drive, my sister and I walk to work, trekking over flat and dusty terrain all the way. Although we eventually found a nice café called Gilbertsen's for breakfast, Allene and I prefer eating fruit and cottage cheese in our room the rest of the time. I think we're losing weight.

Our first show in Barnesville was on the seventh, and wouldn't you know it, right at showtime a fierce wind tore through everything, whipping props and our plywood scenery around but good. Each of us, as we came prancing onstage in the Beach routine with open parasols, got pulled across the boards! Jat said afterward he expected to see us fly away, one by one, up and off the stage. None of the acts had an easy time. Props rolled around and costumes and hairdos came apart. Hazards of working outdoors!

Around midnight, the terrible wind was followed by a violent thunderstorm that woke me up with crashing thunder and spectacular lightning. Mother Nature turned it on loud and clear, and I thought for sure we'd be whisked away by a tornado, like Dorothy on the way to Oz, bed and all. Couldn't believe it. While I trembled under my pillow and sheet, Allene slept right on through.

In contrast, the next day when we did the grandstand show, it was calm, pleasant, and warm, but there were all kinds of bugs—

mosquitoes, beetles, and who-knows-what—swarming around. The footlights attracted them by the hundreds (thousands?), and many died there in heaps of spindly bodies and wings.

This is our last day in Barnesville. Hurray! I can't say I've enjoyed working here, so I'll be glad to leave. It isn't nearly as green and agreeable as Fertile. Again, we don't have far to go to our next fair and have time to kill. Because of the time needed to set up the fair and then tear it down again, we're only performing (and getting paid for) three days a week. That leaves us with nothing to do but sit around the other four days listening to the radio or Penni's record player, not exactly the best way to make a living. One good thing: there's no place to shop and therefore no temptation to spend the little we earn!

Manhattan Models in Charleston costumes with County Fair emcee.

Chapter Thirteen

July 12, 1955

Arrived in Fessenden, North Dakota, on the tenth, after a boring 200-mile drive from Barnesville. It is dry and flat as a tortilla around here, not green like Minnesota with its lakes and trees. We are staying at the Conner Hotel, the only hotel Fessenden has to offer. While it's old and not so great, the Conner is greatly appreciated since we feel lucky to have found a place. Guess it's going to be hit or miss concerning accommodations, and it has occurred to each of us that there may be a time or two when we do not find anywhere to stay and have to sleep in the car! The Herods, and other acts doing the fairs, have the best idea by pulling a trailer to live in, allowing them to just drive onto fairgrounds and "drop anchor" where there's space.

Picked up the mail at General Delivery. Allene and I received a letter from Elaine. She and Pete are buying a home in the Seattle area and will be moving out of Anacortes soon. That's exciting news, but I'll bet Mom and Papa will miss having them nearby.

Penni heard from Peg and Red. They are living and working in Lake Tahoe now. Don't know what Red's doing, but Peg's making good money dancing in one of the big shows. Apparently, Yvonne Moray, a singer we performed with in Portland, Oregon a couple of years ago, is appearing at one of the nightclubs. She and her brother, Emil, helped Peg and Red find jobs so they could stay in Tahoe. Kind of neat.

I remember Yvonne as a tiny, delightful living doll. Entering the dressing room on opening night at Amato's Supper Club in Portland, I stood stunned and staring for a moment. In front of me was a rack full of little, solid-sequined gowns in assorted colors. What a surprise! I knew we'd be sharing space with a singer but not one who is only thirty inches tall! Yvonne did a super act and was so much fun to be around, always chatting and pleasant. She had been one of the Munchkin toe dancers in the movie, *The Wizard of Oz*. She told us how much fun it was to work with so many folks that were as small as she is.

Allene sent money home today ($100) to put toward the house. So far, we've sent a total of $1,650. It may be a while before we can spare any more, as cash is scarce these days. Hope Mom will write soon so we'll have news from home. Since living with bugs, heat, dust, and thunderstorms in the Midwest, I appreciate the Pacific Northwest all the more. Ah, to see a tall, green fir tree dancing in the wind again.

Didn't do a matinee this afternoon. Instead, horse races in front of the grandstand every few minutes were the event of the day. Free for the afternoon, Allene and I took JoAleene through the fair, looking at handicraft exhibits, farm animals, 4-H stuff (everyone's really into that), plus baked goods, flowers, and vegetables, which looked like the heat's got to them. Blue ribbons still hanging off everything. Strolled over to the midway and took a ride on the merry-go-round and the Ferris wheel. I wanted to do the Tilt-a-Whirl, but no one was interested in going with me.

We're beginning to recognize the people who run the rides and concessions, as well as the roustabouts. And it's a nice feeling. The folks in the ticket booths smile and let us through the gate like we're a visiting part owner or favorite relative. The same carnival outfit travels from fair to fair, setting up, tearing down, setting up, tearing down. Hot work. You really have to love it. (Or the pay is awfully good.)

Tonight, the show was held off for twenty minutes while it poured and poured buckets of rain. I felt sorry for all the people, huddled together and patiently waiting in the covered grandstand. To keep them entertained, the high school band in their blue uniforms with gold braid trim, played song after song and medley after medley until the deluge slacked off. We heard everything from John Phillip Sousa to Stephen Foster to Glenn Miller, and the music sounded darn good too.

Of course, it was immediately showtime when the rain finally stopped, and we faced the dubious prospect of working on a soaking-wet stage. As our show band played, the Manhattan Models danced across boards slick as a freshly waxed floor, and it was all we could do to stay upright in our high heels! I slipped plenty but didn't fall. Neither did the others. I think it's a case of bending your knees and hardly picking up your feet, in other words, kind of "mushing" through the dance. Beats taking a pratfall.

July 15, 1955

We are now in the dynamic metropolis of Warren, Minnesota. Although a very small town (sigh), it's still about three times larger than Fessenden. Arrived here two days ago and had a super hard time finding somewhere to live. No motels or hotels. Desperately in need of accommodations, the four of us split up and went from house to house and block to block, knocking on doors, asking for a room, or having people call up their friends. No fun.

Finally got very nice rooms close to the fairgrounds with an angel named Mrs. Filippi. Allene and I then promptly went out and bought our fruit, cereal, and cottage cheese at the Red Owl market. Cafés here don't look so hot; therefore, I know we'll be doing a lot of eating in.

This fair is smaller than the ones we've played thus far, and, walking around the grounds, it was easy to find the Bryants in their booths on opening day. This time, Josie is selling rhinestone setters because another person has the punchboard needlework stand here. Next to her in another booth is Captain Billy with his fountain pens, as usual. I guess he had to contend with some pesty character at the Fessenden fair. He told us this guy bought and broke a pen, then came back for a replacement. The jerk gave Captain Billy such a bad time by coming back repeatedly, that he finally sent him off with a dozen pens in his fist. "God makes 'em and I meet 'em," Captain Billy said, then added, "I was damned glad to tear down and get out of town!"

Saw JoAleene helping both grandparents spread their displays over walls and tables. It's great she is able to spend so much time with the Bryants, setting up or taking over their stands when they need a break. Since JoAleene's their only grandchild, Josie and Billy are more than pleased to have her around. Had to do a matinee yesterday. That is, we performed all afternoon between the ostrich and horse races, which equates to a lot of standing around waiting in the heat and dust. Because doing a show in bits and pieces makes for a long day, none of the acts cares for the spaced-out performance. But, I guess, horses and ostriches need time to catch their breath! I shouldn't complain. The races are fun to watch, especially seeing those gigantic ostriches loping along. Horses galloping by kick up clouds of dust, though, and I know Betty is concerned about what's happening to our costumes.

Did our final grandstand show tonight, and the weather was sensational: nice and warm with a colossal moon and a sky full of stars. All of us performers loved it! Unfortunately, the mosquitoes did too, and were out in full force looking for a meal. We've started using a bug repellent called 6-12 that may or may not even work. These are tough mosquitoes. Also, giant sized. Like bigger than a silver dollar.

July 19, 1955

We are now in Roseau, Minnesota. Had a heck of a time finding somewhere to stay (again). Got into town early last night, and, after discovering that the few hotels in the area were full, drove around house hunting for two hours. Penni and Lori got a room first in a nice home just off the main street. Allene and I felt like rejects until their landlady started calling her friends to find accommodations for us. That took another hour. Fortunately, we ended up in a beautiful home near Penni and Lori. Our landlady is Mrs. Gavelin. After getting moved in, we had dinner at the Encore Café. Pretty good and within walking distance.

Didn't get a lot of sleep during the night because of an extremely noisy thunderstorm with lightning bolts that lit up the whole room. I tried putting the pillow over my head but almost suffocated from the heat. Decided maybe I should stay awake and alert anyway, in case we got struck by lightning, or a tree fell on the house (or something worse), and I'd have to make a run for it. But of course, nothing did. Like before, Allene slept right through the whole thing!

Picked up our mail at General Delivery this morning. Received letters from Francis, Don in Denver, Ray, Cal, and Mom, who says Papa sold the furniture store in Anacortes, so is now officially retired and can do more carpentry at the house. The stone fireplace is in and has tall windows on either side which look out into the trees, she went on, making it seem like living in the woods. Mom mentioned she wants to put her dog picture from England over the mantelpiece but will wait until Allene and I get home (if we ever do) before making a final decision.

It's been a while since Allene heard from Dick, and she was certainly disappointed to find no letter from him today. Of course, the main tourist season in Jackson Hole is in full swing now. I think he must be very busy selling hot dogs and hasn't time to write. Then too, we move a lot, going from fair to fair. (Why am I making up excuses for him?!)

Wasn't surprised to see a lot of junk on the streets and in the gutters of Roseau from last night's storm. We were supposed to do a matinee this afternoon, but, because of the rain, the fairgrounds and racetrack were a muddy mess, according to the Herods, so everything got canceled until evening.

Taking advantage of the sightseeing time suddenly available, a bunch of us drove up to check out the Lake of the Woods, an enormous and beautiful body of water only about twenty miles from Roseau. Optimistic about making a day of it, some of the guys took fishing gear along. Jat, who's never fished before, dropped a line off the end of a pier and caught a five-pound fish in just a couple of minutes! Surprised everyone, especially Jat! Then, Billy Pappin, our emcee, and Dave Workman, who does a balloon act, figured if they rented a boat and went out on the lake, they could get even more fish. The plan was to have a big fish fry at the end of the day. For hours, the rest of us watched and waited on shore before the two came back with sunburns and an empty boat. Betty cooked up the one fish Jat caught and made sandwiches to go around. That had to do for the day's outing and our dinner.

Mud or no mud, we had a good crowd for the grandstand show this evening. Before going onstage for the Gypsy, I stood in the wings to watch the tightrope-walking clown. He does some crazy, exciting stuff, like falling over, dangling from ropes, and acting as though he were drunk. The audience just eats it up, gasping or yelling each time he slips. Since I've noticed he's always smiling like nothing ever bothers him, I got up the nerve to speak with our clown/aerialist afterward. He says he does shows every summer, living in a trailer with his family, hauling around trapeze equipment, and going all over the Midwest from fair to fair. I think this guy, who is a physical ed teacher the rest of the year, is SO cute with his blond crewcut and bulging muscles from head to toe. I asked if I could try swinging on his trapeze sometime between shows, and he said okay. Looks pretty easy and must be fun.

Allene says I'd better be careful—not of the trapeze—of Betty Herod. And my big sister is probably right. Betty will be angry if I get up on high-flying equipment. I'm afraid it's the same old thing. In Billings, when I went horseback riding with a rancher to see his land and cattle, Betty said dancers have no business riding horses. What if I fell and broke something? Same thing with skiing. Shouldn't have tried that up at Mt. Hood when we were booked in Portland. Dancers shouldn't ski. Way too risky. I think the Herods worry too much, although I suppose I can kind of understand their point of view. But I think I should be able to have some fun sometime.

We've gotten to know a couple of the fellows who do the setting up and tearing down. Their names are Mike and Bob, and they say they are roustabouts during the summer to earn money for college. Bob is from Ohio, very much into jazz, and worships Stan Kenton. (I think Lori kind of goes for him.) He is tall, blond, and very good-looking. He's getting a good tan too, probably because of so much idle time between setups and teardowns. Mike has dark hair, green eyes, and is even taller than Bob, but on the quiet side. I think he's from Maine. Penni hangs around him while Lori's with Bob. They all can talk about college things, I guess.

This evening I heard Mike say his favorite ride was the Tilt-a-Whirl, same as me, so I told him so. Then, when everyone was talking about the bad thunderstorm that canceled our matinee, I piped up and said I thought we were lucky it hadn't rained during any other shows so far. Mike chimed in saying that, different from roustabouts like himself who routinely set up or tear down in the rain, show people never get wet. It just doesn't rain during performances; therefore, performers must be very lucky or charmed. Well, I had to go ahead and bet Mr. Smart Guy a ride on the Tilt-a-Whirl that one day the entertainers would get soaked trying to do a show.

July 24, 1955

Arrived here in Mahnomen two days ago. It was the first day of the fair, but we didn't have to do a show because of the camel and ostrich races. Got a room easily, this time, because Josie Bryant reserved them for us with friends of hers, the Agnews, in their nice, old house. Penni, Lori, Allene, and I really appreciated driving into town without worrying about finding a place to live.

Yesterday, Allene and I visited JoAleene over on the midway. Although she's been scooping up snow cones or selling tickets for Kiddie Kar rides, the Herods' daughter is now at the merry-go-round, making sure kids are strapped to the poles. She likes this job best of all. By now, she knows most of the vendors, the people in charge of the rides, and the hawkers. She is right at home anywhere on the fairgrounds. These small jobs—plus helping the Bryants from time to time—keep JoAleene occupied and happy. It provides a nice change. Better than sitting backstage in a smoky old nightclub playing with dolls.

Once the merry-go-round started moving, JoAleene came over to say hello. She told us they almost lost Cheekaboom on the last trip! When the Herods were packing up to leave Roseau, the dog was outside the trailer, and they forgot all about her. An hour and several miles later, Betty discovered Cheeka was missing, so they quickly turned around and went back to the fairgrounds. Lucky for them (and the little dog), Cheekaboom was sitting alone in the huge, completely empty field where the Herods' trailer had been parked, just waiting. Smart little dog.

Our first grandstand show in Mahnomen went very well last night. The evening was warm and lovely, with only a faint breeze to stir up tiny funnels of dirt. Would have been perfect if it weren't for the darn bugs all over the place.

Each morning we've been in Mahnomen I wake up to the lovely smell of something baking. It's our landlady, Mrs. Agnew, downstairs in the kitchen making doughnuts. I've never seen anyone do that before, because Mom never fixed us anything in deep fat and we rarely ate doughnuts.

Anyway, responding to the delicious aroma, I've been rushing downstairs to watch how easily Mrs. Agnew does the job, shaping and turning each doughnut so perfectly. She's never offered me even one, though. I do my best to look absolutely starving, but so far it hasn't worked. What does she do with all those doughnuts? (Aha, she's supplying fair food booths!)

Walked over to the fairgrounds today to hunt up my clown friend and find out if I could hang around on his trapeze. Allene came with me "to pick up the pieces," she said. Found Jerry—that's his name—tightening some of the wires holding the rig, which really isn't very high off the ground. I saw that I'd swing about one hundred feet across from one platform to the other. Simple enough—and it was okay with Jerry.

While a few people watched, I climbed the rope ladder to the platform, about twenty feet off the ground. Jerry handed me the swing and told me to hold it over my head, then just fall forward off the platform. I took a deep breath and off I went, falling down, down, down like I would crash into the ground. My shoulders ached horribly, and my arms felt like they were being pulled from their sockets! The pain was such a surprise and so awful, I thought I couldn't hang on. But I did. I swooped lazily, silently, slowly (too slowly for me) over the turf and landed shaken, but otherwise all right, on the opposite platform. Even heard the faint patter of sparse applause from onlookers. Unfortunately, standing next to my grim-faced sister, I saw Betty glaring at me over tightly folded arms. Oops.

We do another show tonight, then that's it for about a week. I think Penni will want to go someplace before our next fair, maybe to visit Joann in Indiana.

July 26, 1955

The four of us stayed one extra day in Mahnomen so we could relax and sunbathe in the Agnew's backyard, unconcerned about doing a show or anything else. Even took turns mowing their big lawn that goes all around the house. Kind of neat. Since we have a week off, Penni decided we should go to Madison, Wisconsin to check it out and stay a couple of days. Then drive to Indiana to visit Joann. Our friend has just opened a dancing school in Anderson. Sounds good.

Packed and left Mahnomen yesterday afternoon, while skies were still sunny and temps pretty warm. Penni figured, since we were going all the way to Madison, she should drive through Minneapolis at midnight to beat the heat and traffic. Surprise, surprise, she didn't beat either one. When we arrived at that time, the metropolis was hot, humid, and horrible, with cars and people everywhere. Minneapolis looked something like New Orleans at Mardi Gras, except no one was having any fun! Poor people. Hundreds wandered zombie-like around in shorts or bathing suits, while others stretched out on towels and blankets in the grass trying to sleep. So much for traveling through the city in the cool of the evening.

After stopping at Gable's in Richland for a nice early-morning breakfast of poached eggs and toast, we arrived in Madison and found a great place to stay on a tree-lined street. Unpacked some, then went out for some wonderful ice cream at a dairy. It really hit the spot and was creamier than most ice creams you can buy in a store.

Although sizzling hot and almost unbearable, the city of Madison's also fantastically green and clean. The four of us like it here very much—a wonderful change from county fair dust, wind, and bugs! We'll probably spend at least one more day doodling around before going to Joann's for the rest of our week off. I hope the Herods are enjoying some days of leisure up at Lake of the Woods where they planned to camp and maybe catch another fish.

*Pat and Allene
in sombreros for
a Mexican hat
dance, 1955.*

*Allene and Pat in
costume for their tap
dance speciality at
The Cave Supper Club,
Vancouver, B.C., 1954.*

Chapter Fourteen

July 29, 1955

We are now in East Dubuque, Illinois. While we were in Madison, Penni called the Herods' agent in Chicago to report our whereabouts and found out we open at the Hilltop Casino tonight for two weeks! So here we are, and it is opening night. Don't know what happened. So much for our week off. Didn't even get to Indiana to see Joann.

Because funds are running low for each of us, it's just as well we didn't have the full week off. We're not doing that many county fairs and, therefore, not making our usual salary. JoAleene told Penni that her parents, although enjoying the carefree life with the trailer, were concerned about the situation too. The fairs are not enough. We're lucky the Hilltop could take us! It's one of the few clubs the Herods can depend upon to regularly book the revue.

Like Jat's been saying for about a year, a six-person act is getting too expensive for the small clubs. Penni said our "spy" would not tell more, except that we need to work harder, all of us, at looking prettier, dancing better, and cleaning up any sloppiness. Maybe Jat thinks he can get us booked on the hotel circuit. Their ballrooms are top notch and hotel managers could easily afford us, but I'm pretty sure they demand classy acts with gorgeous costumes. That would take lots of work, promotion, and money.

Allene was quite upset to hear all the bad news. How can my sister do more to improve when she tries so hard already with diets, exercise, new costumes, new cocktail dresses, furs, jewelry, and everything else she does to look and be at her best? My sister takes things very seriously. Not like Penni and Lori, who sort of shrug their shoulders, obviously not that concerned about dancing for a living. If the revue folds, so what? They'll go back to college. We don't have that option.

This is the third time Allene and I have worked the Hilltop Casino in East Dubuque. I think it's a favorite with all of us. For one thing, the Manhattan Models get to live in the little house on the hill near the club. It's kind of isolated and in the woods. Walking home at night after work is a bit spooky, but during the day, it's heaven! Very quiet and pleasant, plus we have a great view of the Mississippi River with Dubuque, Iowa, on the other side. And, since there's never anyone around, we can sunbathe with little or nothing on to get nice, even tans minus bathing suit lines.

For another thing, the band at the Hilltop is excellent. They've played our show music so often they don't need a rehearsal. Plus, Betty uses Bunny Dillon, the resident piano player, to write any new musical arrangements for us, because he's fast, good, and not expensive. The club also features great food and caters to reliable, regular customers who come weekly for dinner and the show. Besides all that, the Hilltop Casino has the distinction of being the model for Ross and Adler's song, "Hernando's Hideaway," from their hit musical, The Pajama Game, which is set in Dubuque. Anyway, it is indeed a special place.

The opening went well tonight—but I had to laugh. First, Roger, Penni's boyfriend, came by the house after work to see if we had arrived all right. Then, the club owners, Mr. and Mrs. Harrington, drove up to check doors and windows to make sure we were safe. After that, the police in their squad car came up, parked, and skimmed the woods with headlights, a searchlight, and flashlights! We're very well taken care of here.

August 1, 1955

Betty has taken an interest in our singing act again. She wants Allene and me to practice extra hard in order to whip our routines into shape during this engagement, so we are doing two spots in this week's lineup—first and third shows. The first show is the Halliday Twins strongest act, and we wear our newest and prettiest outfits— the snazzy white costumes loaded with beaded snowflakes and fringe. Everything went fine the first two nights at the club, then, last night I had some trouble. Real trouble. When Jat introduced the "singing, dancing Halliday Twins" the music began, and Allene strode confidently into the spotlight. I followed right behind—and promptly fell on my back with my feet in the air! My breakaway skirt, fastened with snaps, broke away, leaving me with an open slit up the back from my knees to my waist. Fortunately, the beaded leotard underneath was intact. Wasn't much I could do but scramble to my feet and go through the act with my costume half off. Pretty bad—and a total distraction for us, the band, the audience, and everybody else. I think I know what happened. The floor was a little slippery, plus the big taps on my shoes don't leave me much shoe leather to walk on.

I'm sure Betty must have seen it. She watches our act every night so she can give us pointers, but she didn't say a thing about my total no-one-could-possibly-have-missed debacle. Probably she hasn't any advice for a person with small feet and big taps.

Today is Monday and our day off at the Hilltop Casino. We were supposed to drive over to Donnellson, Iowa to do the county fair grandstand show, but everything got canceled. Seems they've had an outbreak of polio in the area, causing public affairs and places like parks and swimming pools to be closed down. Pretty dismal for those people. Making the most of the schedule change, Allene and I planned to bleach our hair first thing after breakfast. Reacting to brilliant sunshine and blue skies, my sister came up with one of her great ideas: let's take advantage of the glorious weather and do the job outside. Sounded good, so I set up a chair and table behind the house. That way Allene could enjoy the view of the Mississippi while I applied the smelly goop to her roots. What we both forgot to consider was the lovely, daily breeze that always blows up from the river. Had a time keeping her hair from flying around while I sectioned it off to apply the bleach. Another problem: pesty gnats crawling or falling into the foam! Defeated from start to finish with

Allene's hair, we went inside when it was my turn to be done. Only good thing about bleaching hair outside—NO smell.

Got a call from Betty wanting to rehearse over at the club in the afternoon, so we met her there after lunch. Apparently she is anxious to work up some new routines for us to break in as soon as possible. Today, we started on a sisters' medley which will use tunes done by The Boswell, Andrews, and McGuire Sisters as well as Patience and Prudence. Since we can't sound like any of them, we'll be doing comedy takeoffs on their famous hits.

Allene thinks the reason Betty is moving so fast has to do with the availability of Bunny Dillon, the pianist/arranger at the Hilltop. Although our boss can throw new routines at us as fast as we can pick them up, it's getting the musical arrangements written that holds up breaking in a new number. Therefore, having Bunny right here, ready, willing, and able, throws the creation of new numbers into high gear.

That evening, since we didn't go to Donnellson to work the fair, the whole revue was invited to a barbecue dinner over in Dubuque. We had sixteen-ounce sirloin steaks, baked potatoes, salad, and corn on the cob. Lots of people were there, and we sat outdoors eating and swatting bugs at the same time. It was kind of funny. The host doing the barbecuing saw me finish off the whole steak dinner in record time and jokingly asked me if I'd like another. I said, "Sure!" and ended up eating another big steak dinner while everyone laughed—except the Herods. Guess I embarrassed them.

August 5, 1955

Got a letter from Mom today. She writes that stuff we've sent home, like souvenirs and photos, has been piling up in boxes all over the place. Now that the house is in shape, she plans to put them into scrapbooks and hang some on the walls for visitors to see. No news from anybody else. I guess they don't know where we are. Allene really misses news from Dick and has written him from here, but before you know it, we'll be gone again doing fairs.

Interesting events tonight! During the first show, because our dressing room is next to the bar, we had barflies who were more interested in grabbing a peek at us changing every time the door opened than in watching the floor show. Betty complained to the bartender, who complained to Mr. Harrington, who promptly planted his wife, Tess, a pretty good-sized lady, at a table in front of the dressing room door like a guard. Anyone stealing a glance in that direction got a dirty look. That finished that problem.

Then, just before the second show, Jat, all flustered and out of breath, came rushing into the dressing room. He'd heard a tip-off that the Hilltop would be robbed tonight and wanted all of us to vacate the premises—fast! Threw robes on over our costumes. Grabbed purses and makeup kits. Ran out into the parking lot. Waited quietly, huddled together in the Herods' station wagon in the dark, watching and listening for trouble. Didn't see anything. And all we heard was a chorus of crickets. The police came, of course, parked, and sat waiting just like us. But nothing happened. So, after an hour's delay, we finally went back into the club and did the second show.

Except for Betty, all the rushing around for nothing was no big deal. Unfortunately, she had turned too quickly trying to get out the club's front door and backed right into a table edge, injuring her hip. While we sat in the station wagon waiting to see a cops and robbers show, Betty couldn't do anything but wiggle from side to side, changing positions to keep weight off her tailbone. Because of the pain, she even tried turning around and leaning over the front seat.

The highlight of our second show is the Old Lady Bit, where Jat first sings with two band members as part of a trio called the Shed House Three. One of the dancers walks onstage swinging a tiny purse which she drops in front of one of the trio. He picks up the purse and hands it to the girl, who opens it up and exclaims, "All my life savings, and you didn't touch a penny. Just for that, you can meet me 'round the corner in a half an hour. Meet me 'round the corner in a half an hour." She walks offstage swinging her purse followed by that trio member. Jat then announces, "You will now hear from the Shed House Two." They begin to sing as another dancer walks onstage swinging her little purse and drops it in front of the two singers. The routine is repeated with the singer picking up her purse, etc., and Jat is left to sing alone. Betty then comes onstage as a dumpy old lady with a huge handbag that she drops on Jat's foot, and the two do about fifteen minutes of gags. At the end, Betty does encore after encore of eccentric dancing. The Old Lady Bit is surefire every performance and is Betty's special number. Got the shock of my life tonight when Jat approached me to take her place! The conversation went something like this:

"Betty hurts too much, can hardly stand, and certainly can't dance."
"But me? Why me?"
"You've heard the routine for two years and know the lines by now."
"But . . ."
"I think you can do the dance too."
"But . . ."
"You're short and well, kind of, well, I know you can get the laughs."
"Oh."

So, halfway through the second show as Jat was telling some lead-in jokes to the Old Lady Bit and Betty sat on a pillow smiling faintly at me, I put on her baggy dress, high-button shoes, glasses, tattered fur piece, and slouch hat. Still in shock, I strolled out into the spotlight, on cue, and became the old lady and the butt of Jat's one-liners, like: "What have we here? A creature from outer space or the bride of Frankenstein?" and "You've heard of The Lost Weekend. Well, I think I found it."

I went through the bit, automatically supplying the punch lines. I was Betty, mouthing her responses, getting her laughs. If I'd had time to rehearse and actually think about what I was doing, I would have lost my voice and collapsed from jelly knees, for sure. As it happened, I did two encores and was shaking with excitement when I got back to the dressing room. Received pats on the back from Betty, Penni, Lori, and Allene. Guess they'd been watching with the dressing room door opened a crack.

But this strange evening wasn't over. After the last show, Allene and I started walking up the hill to the house. It was awfully dark, except for neat little fireflies swirling all around, lighting up and going out, lighting up and going out, helping us to see. Soon, however, we noticed headlights coming up behind us. Allene and I quickly slipped into bushes by the side of the road, ducked down, and watched. Two unfamiliar men in a maroon Chevrolet passed us and continued up our driveway. So, this was why so many friends checked on us that first day back!

Cutting through the woods, Allene and I ran the rest of the way to the dark house, sneaked inside through the back, then, without turning on any lights, peered out the window. The strange car came slowly up to the front door and stopped. Because we passed him coming and going from our dressing room during the show, I recognized one of these guys as a barfly who'd been snatching glances of us.

The two creeps started to get out of the Chevy but were interrupted by another car coming up the grade. Right away, the engine fired up, and the Chevy beat it right back down the hill. The latest arrivals turned out to be Penni and Lori in the old Plymouth. I think I was never so glad to see those two! Feeling safe and secure at last, the four of us sat around the kitchen table in our nightshirts, snacking on celery, apples, cheese, and salami. All of a sudden we heard shots—three of them—from the direction of the club's parking lot. Penni jumped up and flipped out the lights. We sat very still at the kitchen table in the dark, holding our breaths and waiting, waiting, waiting. But everything stayed quiet. No more shots, no sounds at all.

About one minute later, a police car came roaring up the driveway and slammed to a halt in a gravel-spraying skid. Two officers hopped out, guns in hand, and ran in opposite directions into the woods. Afraid of what we might see or hear, Penni, Lori, Allene, and I, nonetheless, watched bobbing flashlights between trees and bushes below the house. Eventually, one of the policemen came to the front door to see if we were all right. It was Jiggs, a cop we knew from the last time we played the Hilltop. Having found nothing and being assured we were fine, both officers drove off.

The quiet darkness seemed suffocating. Adding to the eerie feeling, lightning flashed all around—no thunder or rain—just lightning. None of us could sleep, so we sat in the kitchen eating raisins, while discussing Peeping Toms, prowlers in the woods, prune diets, and old boyfriends.

August 11, 1955

Last night during our act in the first show, while Allene and I were singing, we were startled as a drunk came lurching and staggering into the spotlight, took one look at us, then fell on his face right at our feet! Allene and I kept singing, although I don't think anyone was paying attention to us. In fact, the audience was laughing at this poor guy, out cold on the dance floor! While we continued with our act, Mr. Harrington dragged the drunk off the stage to a round of applause.

During the third show, the Halliday Twins broke in two new routines: a medley of songs about Ohio (which included "Down by the Ohio") and Kay Starr's version of Harry Woods's popular oldie, "Side by Side," to make sure sequences and repeats are what the Herods want. Bunny, our piano player who did the arrangements, could make any changes easily enough, but everything was fine. Now he can go ahead and add more instrument parts.

Today, we had a rehearsal with Betty to trim the act's rough edges and beef up the gestures. Because she feels we need more clarity and feeling when we sing lyrics, she brought along a book of poems by Robert Service for Allene and me to read aloud, concentrating on clear pronunciation and emotion. After that, we ran through a bunch of our songs to add "more clarity and feeling" to all of them. It was pretty grueling.

Then, Betty suggested we get some gags in our act and try some patter between songs. That, she said, should give us both some personality and get us closer to the audience. Betty's choice is a short vaudeville routine. Goes like this:

Allene: *"Some people can't tell Pat and me apart—after all, we're twins—but it's really very simple. You see, I'm the sophisticated one."*
Pat: *With a giggle, "I'm the little cute one you don't have to spend much money on."*
Allene: *"I design all the costumes, do all the choreography, select all*

of our songs, and do all the musical arrangements."
Pat*: With a giggle, "I'm the little cute one you don't have to spend much money on."*
Allene*: "I handle all the bookings, accommodations, and transportation."*
Pat*: "I'm . . ."*
Allene*: Turns and shouts, "STOP THAT, PAT!"*
Pat*: Freezes. Her eyes go crossed. She cannot get them uncrossed until Allene gives her a hard shove that knocks her away from the microphone.*

We practiced and practiced. Allene and I had no voices left by the time we quit!

Early this evening, before the first show, there was a party for JoAleene. Dee Cross, the lady from the furriers, set it up, did the decorations, and invited children JoAleene's age for ice cream, cake, and presents. It was a big, wonderful birthday party. And boy, did all the kids have fun! Dee's such a great person. She does this for JoAleene every time the Herods work East Dubuque and the Hilltop Casino.

Right after the second show tonight, there was a fight outside the club with all kinds of yelling and people smacking one another. I wasn't scared. In fact, the front door was open, and sitting at the bar, I had a ringside seat to watch the excitement. A woman standing too close, trying to see everything, got hit in the nose and had blood running down her face. After that, Jat, playing the hero, pulled two guys apart who were battling it out and nearly got punched by one of them. Then Betty, furious that Jat got involved, grabbed his arm and pulled him back just as another man swung at his head. I saw Jiggs, the policeman, handcuff a shaggy-looking man, who was spitting mad, and shove him into the squad car. Someone later commented that Jiggs had come to arrest the prowler who'd been in the woods, and that confrontation had started the brawl!

Had to laugh. Despite all the noise outside, John, a regular customer at the Hilltop, slept through the whole thing. It seems this guy often drinks too much and nods off while standing at the bar.

When the bartender hears snoring, he'll routinely reach over and put John's hand on the rail so he won't fall and hurt himself. If I hadn't been sitting at the bar and seen him, I wouldn't have believed anyone could sleep standing up. Through a fight, yet!

During our act in the third show, Allene and I broke in the comedy patter we'd been rehearsing this afternoon. Allene has so many lines to remember, while I only have one: "I'm the little cute one you don't have to spend much money on." And I blew it. My mind went blank. Having only a vague idea of what it should be, I blurted out, "I'm the little cute one that doesn't cost very much." The audience gasped. All the way from the dressing room, I could hear Betty, Penni, and Lori roaring with laughter. And I couldn't get it right! Three times I said, loud and clear, "I'm the little cute one that doesn't cost very much." I felt my face burning; I was so embarrassed. Oddly enough, people did laugh, probably realizing I'd messed up the bit. I appreciated that tad of sympathy. Allene was so wrapped up in getting her own lines right, she didn't notice I'd messed up.

All in all, it was a fitting last night at the Hilltop Casino. There is no more club work in sight for us. Jat is trying to book one-nighters (anywhere he can get them) to pad our skinny pocketbooks between fair dates.

August 16, 1955

A few days ago, although still living in East Dubuque, we drove over to Waukon, Iowa, to do a county fair. We just stayed the day and did one show, which went very well, with the grandstand filled to capacity.

Because she's nuts about him, Lori went looking for Bob, the fair roustabout, as soon as we arrived in Waukon. He really is cute, but seems a little too confident about his gorgeous smile and pretty blue eyes. I'll bet he has lots of girlfriends. Penni agrees. She said she jokingly told Lori that Bob's a "real heartbreaker," but doesn't think our new girl picked up the message. I get the feeling Lori's more than willing to play Bob's love-'em-and-leave-'em game. Anyway, Bob didn't disappoint Lori. He was Johnny-on-the-spot, running to meet her, bubbling over at the sight of her, and Lori ate it up, of course.

During the grandstand show, our new girl exhibited rare form, laughing at just about everything, bouncing around, but not quite with the rest of us doing the Charleston. Allene accidentally kicked her in the face (not very hard, thank goodness!) because Lori wasn't where she should have been. Although she didn't forget the steps, she was not keeping up. It was like she couldn't move fast enough. None of this peculiar stuff escaped Betty's watchful eye, but she didn't say a thing. As we all expected, Lori disappeared fast after the closing number. Penni, Allene, and I were held up an hour waiting for her. Stood around the parking lot watching other people come and go until our smitten comrade came swooping across to the car, drinking champagne out of a Dixie cup! Apparently, too much of the bubbly was her problem all evening because, when we got back to the house in East Dubuque, Lori threw up as she opened the car door. Wonderful. Penni had to put her to bed.

The next night, we did a club date across the river in Dubuque. The show was very well received, even though, I'm sure, most of the group had seen us at the Hilltop Casino at least once or twice. Didn't matter. We know they really love us here, because, in addition, we were given a lovely dinner of delicious chicken, corn, biscuits, and peach pie. However, what should have been an exceptionally great evening got spoiled.

Just as we were packing up costumes and props to leave, Jat told us to stop what we were doing. He sat down and lit a cigarette—then calmly dropped a BOMB! Seems he has made up his mind to go back to Europe! Bookings in this country, Jat said, are too hard to come by. Can't work fifty weeks a year and make money like we used to, because clubs are either closing or cutting back entertainment. We're up against stars like Bob Hope and Jack Benny on TV shows that an audience can watch either at home or in a bar, he went on to say. With fewer and fewer clubs presenting regular nightly floor shows, acts have little to look forward to for jobs and need to travel greater distances to pick up precious bookings. In short, the bottom's fallen out of the US nightclub circuit.

Penni started chewing on her nails, which had only recently begun to look normal again. Lori heaved a sigh, shifted her weight, and folded her arms, while Allene and I went back to packing costumes.

Jat went on. Each of us is welcome to come along to Europe. But, our boss went on to say, it's a whole new area. He doesn't know the clubs or the agents. There would be no guarantees of work or pay. We might even need to split up to keep working. But, Jat added, he thinks an American show should do okay.

While slipping on her shoes, Betty put in her two bits by saying that the revue could stay in the United States and scrounge for bookings, accepting anything, and hope to survive as a unit that way—or we could travel overseas where the show would be, she was certain, a novelty. But Europe's a long way to go on a gamble, Betty had to admit. Anyway, she offered the Manhattan Models this advice: from here on out, we should save as much money as possible whether we opt to go overseas with them or not.

Penni, Lori, Allene, and I started back across the river to East Dubuque in darkness and heavy silence. There was nothing to discuss anyway. I thought about what JoAleene had told us earlier concerning the show's booking problems. Should have known something ominous was cooking. Just then, as if Mother Nature had to add to our dismal feelings, thunder growled at us, lightning bolts attacked all around, and rain pounded down on the old Plymouth.

Chapter Fifteen

August 23, 1955

Left East Dubuque about a week ago around midnight. I had managed to catch a doozy of a cold our last day there, so, while packing, took time out to gargle with warm salt water, plus smear on some Vicks VapoRub. Still, my eyes watered and my nose dripped constantly all the way to Culbertson, Nebraska, our next job.

We traveled all night and the next day. I felt so lousy, I thought we'd never get there. Stopped to eat at Dixon's in Omaha, then dropped south to Hastings where we ate again at the local Jack n' Jill's. As usual, Allene and I bought fresh fruit at a market, this time Safeway, before resuming the trip. We figure it's always best to have provisions since there may be little available in Culbertson. And we were right! It came as no surprise that our next county fair town turned out to be another wide spot in the road, except emptier and quieter than the others. Arriving in the late afternoon, we felt lucky to find a home with rooms to rent. While the others went for something to eat, I went right to bed and slept fourteen hours. That took care of my cold.

The next day Penni, Lori, Allene, and I checked out Culbertson and discovered this tiny, lonely town on the sprawling prairie has a population of 770. We drove through the city center in a minute and then out to the fairgrounds, which were darn easy to find. The trucks with the carnival rides had already been unloaded, and the guys were busy setting up. Saw Mike and managed to catch his attention long enough to say hello. Since I hadn't seen him in over three weeks and three days, I didn't feel I was being too forward. He and Bob were really busy working on an electrical something that had gone dead.

Mike smiled quickly over his shoulder. Hot as the weather is—and the work—he had no shirt on, so I observed nice muscles and a good tan. But his jeans looked like they were falling off his backside. I didn't want to hang around. Whatever was wrong with the wiring had to be fixed before the gates opened. That's show biz!

Because there was nowhere in Culbertson to eat, the four of us drove over to nearby McCook for dinner at a café called Larry's. We are really out in the wide-open spaces with nothing to see down either side of the highway. No trees or bushes or anything. Yet, for sure, some people manage to live here all the time. I guess they never look out the window or don't mind seeing brown everywhere.

We did only one show—an evening performance—in Culbertson. As might be expected, a warm, dusty wind whistled across the fairgrounds the whole time, getting in our hair, up our noses, and into our mouths if we weren't careful. Lovely. But I shouldn't complain. With so much breeziness, there were fewer bugs to swat.

Having no good reason to hang around, Penni packed up the Plymouth early, and we left that funny little town by midnight. Can't blame her for wanting to make our jumps only at night when it's slightly cooler. We're certainly not missing any scenery. Even at that, jobs are so far apart that Penni's still driving when the sun's up, and, boy, is it unbearable even with the windows open!

Rolled into Sioux City, Iowa, stopping at Martin's Coffee Shop to eat and just walk around awhile. Nice to be in a place with parks, green lawns, theaters, hotels, stores, and shops. Saw the Jackson Hotel where we had stayed, and the big auditorium used for the auto show but didn't recognize much else. The city looks quite different without February's snow and ice.

Arrived in Slayton, Minnesota, thirteen hours after leaving Culbertson, and rented rooms at Mrs. Knoll's, a nice home close to town, then went to a good place for eating called The Hub. We located the fairgrounds and checked on showtimes, then went back to the room and slept until the next morning.

Got up early and had breakfast at The Hub before strolling over to the post office to pick up our mail. Allene received letters from Don in Denver, Cal, Ron, and a card from Kalantan. Nothing from Dick. Penni heard from Peg. She and Red are unemployed again. The club in Tahoe where Peg worked as a dancer expected her to drink it up with the customers every night, and she wouldn't go for that, so quit. I'm sure Red had something to say about it too.

Slayton's near the borders of South Dakota and Iowa. A nice little town, except, like everywhere else, *very* warm. But the surrounding green fields, heat or no heat, contribute to a comfortable, friendly atmosphere, and I appreciate that. It's too bad we couldn't have stayed longer. However, we did just one show and packed up again.

Before leaving Slayton, Betty told Penni, Lori, Allene, and me they are planning to sail on October 19 for England. A letter from London, confirming a contract to do camp shows beginning November 12 and lasting sixteen weeks, is supposedly on its way. At least it's a start. Between the two of them, the Herods can easily do a thirty-minute act, presenting plenty of singing, dancing, comedy, and music.

After East Dubuque and performing in a club again, not to mention doing rehearsals to improve what we have so far for an act, both Allene and I are feeling a bit low. Do we have a future in the entertainment business? We know that county fairs are not for us. We didn't leave home, join a show, and spend time and money building an act to end up battling bugs and heat on the prairie. Sure isn't the show business of glamour and glitter we had in mind! But is that all Allene and I can look forward to if we stay in the United States? Should we scour the country for bookings? Or go overseas and take a chance? Or chuck it all and begin new careers? We really have too much tied up in costumes and music to quit show business altogether, but one way or the other, we'll have to make up our minds soon.

Allene hasn't said much on the subject. Apart from our act, I know she's thinking about Dick and when she'll see him again. If we go to Europe, who knows when we'd come back. Well, nothing—not the sail date or the contract—is actually set yet. Maybe the Herods will change their minds.

Packed up two days later and left Slayton during the evening. Drove to Grand Island, Nebraska, arriving at daybreak yesterday morning. Already, it was terribly hot. We'd have been there sooner, but the radiator boiled over and Penni had to give the Plymouth a rest. Fortunately, we were near a gas station when it happened, and we could park under some trees for a while. I wished and wished so hard it would just rain and cool things off, but that didn't occur. Had breakfast at the Cornhusker Café, then found an air-conditioned motel near the fairgrounds to stay in. (Heaven!) The fair started today, August 23. Instead of doing a regular matinee, we did our dance routines between the horse races, just like in Warren. Sweaty, dusty work with a lot of standing around in between. I just hope the horses appreciated it.

It was the Herods' thirteenth wedding anniversary, so a celebration of sorts took place in the afternoon at their trailer. Penni, Lori, Allene, and I gave them a set of heavy plastic dishes we hope they'll be able to use. Should prove handy as long as they live in the teardrop. Everyone in the show came. Even Gene Holter, owner of the ostriches and camels, showed up in Arab garb with his crew. Betty served only cake and pop for refreshments, but I think everyone had a good time. It's not often the whole group of entertainers comes together for anything.

August 26, 1955

Left Grand Island a couple of nights ago after our last show, and drove north, stopping at Stanley Corners, our favorite little crossroads café. They're open twenty-four hours, and we've pulled into their parking lot three times now, going back and forth between fairs. The waiters and waitresses, as well as the cook, know us and are a neat crew that's always pleasant, despite the hour we drop in. By now, they remember our names, what we usually order on our hamburgers, and how we like them done! The place is right where several highways converge, but is never very busy, probably because we so often arrive in the wee small hours.

After driving 500 miles, we arrived in Alexandria, Minnesota, and checked into the Lake Motor Hotel, a very nice place. Found a Piggly Wiggly within walking distance, so Allene and I replenished our supply of fruit. The surrounding countryside is really pretty with lakes, rolling hills, and lots of trees. Unfortunately, we stayed only one day in Alexandria and didn't work the scheduled matinee because the Herods and some of the other acts were late arriving. Horse races all afternoon was the order of the day instead.

Had a magic act with us for the evening show (something different), and standing backstage, I was able to see how the magician sawed his wife in half. Ha! I still wouldn't care to be part of that trick.

We are now in Appleton, Minnesota, and the show we're working with is terrific! Most of the acts were on the Canadian tour, but since that finished, they have joined our show. Anyway, we now have the three Goetsche Brothers from Switzerland. They perform such stunts as one playing the violin while standing on the head of one of his brothers who rides a unicycle. In another trick, all three are on the unicycle, one atop the other. I think they've probably been doing this stuff since they were very little and may have even grown up in a circus. Then there's Pegleg Bates, the one-legged tap dancer. He's remarkable, doing just about anything a dancer with two legs could do—but better. Never missing a beat, he works easily and naturally with the pegleg. In one part of his act, there is no music, only the syncopated blend of *tap, thump, tap, thump*. The audience goes wild! He has to close each performance. No other act can follow him.

Billy Pappin, the harmonica-playing emcee, is still part of the show, as well as Dave and his balloon act, plus a family with a baby gorilla that rides a tricycle. Because of so many added entertainers, we now have a darn big show.

Last week, Allene wrote home concerning the Herods' plan to leave the country. Then today, feeling enough time had passed for ideas and discussion, Allene called Mom regarding what she and Papa think about our leaving the States and living in Europe. Papa wants us to come home right now, Mom said, and look into other ways to earn a living. He fears something bad might happen to us in foreign countries. Mom agrees. She feels Allene and I should remain in this country, stay in show business, and try for club bookings or television variety shows. Surely, she said, we can call someone like Ed Sullivan and get some work. Allene laughed after she hung up. We'll have to think some more.

My sister and I talked a bit. Allene said that if we follow Papa's advice, we'd be throwing in the towel and wasting our investment. If we followed Mom's advice, we'd need to buy new pictures and a car to get started on our own. But at least we'd be in the States working on the survival of the Halliday Twins, not off with the Herods, barnstorming in strange places. Then, I mentioned that we really don't know much about getting bookings. We've only heard how it works. There's a certain knack, a way to handle agents, like wearing expensive clothes and furs to impress them, bragging about the jobs you've worked and how busy you are with bookings. It's kind of a game. The idea is to appear not to need a job, when, of course, you do. The agent knows what you're up to, therefore you must play the game or you're green—and no one wants to be green.

We kicked that thought around awhile, then agreed that, because of their many years of experience, the Herods *know* how to get bookings. So, just to be safe, Allene decided we should go ahead with passport applications. Sounds good.

August 29, 1955

Found out Penni recently made up her mind too. For sure, she will go with the Herods because she wants to see Europe. Her parents wholeheartedly approve of her decision. The experience, they say, should "broaden her viewpoint and perspective" in preparation for the time she hangs up her dancing shoes and settles down into Seattle society.

Lori talked this big decision over with her parents. They urged her to stay with the group, saying if she were to give up this opportunity, she would probably regret it no matter how great Bob is. They suggested that she could try Europe for a few months, then, if it's really love, she'll know for sure. Not completely convinced, Lori agreed to her parents' plan.

Once the big shall-we-stay-or-shall-we-go-along decision had been made by the four of us, we drove over to Benson, which has a courthouse, to begin the paperwork for passports.

After attending to the passport business, the four of us spent a nice afternoon in Benson, eating ice cream under a huge tree in a little park and talking about things we want to do in Europe. We all want to see Paris! Lori's eyes lit up when we talked about that fabulous place. I think she's warming up to the idea.

Back in Appleton, we went over to the Herods' for dinner. Betty invited the four of us for spaghetti in order to break in her new dishes, and was just putting fruit, cheese, and antipasto outside on the picnic table when a thunderstorm blew in. Boy, all of a sudden, the rain pelted down like a tropical squall! We grabbed the food platters and our plates, then bolted for the dressing room under the grandstand.

Because it poured and poured without letup, we sat around eating our spaghetti dinner under the grandstand. Soon other acts came in for shelter too. It was kind of funny. Everyone sat around looking at one another for about two hours waiting for the rain to stop, all of us wondering if the show would be canceled since, as usual, we were obligated to perform on an outside stage.

Listening to the downpour, one of the acts from Canada recalled an experience he had years ago. He performed a novelty act with a circus in Europe during the war, and, as circuses do, they moved from town to town every few days. One time while traveling, the wagon this trouper drove, with all his equipment and props, got separated from the rest. Like now, heavy rain pounded down. Unable to see very far, he figured he made a wrong turn because soon tanks, big guns, and German soldiers came into view. His wagon was quickly surrounded by the army and searched. No bother! Our world-traveling performer pulled out his juggling and magic tricks to entertain the troops from the back of his wagon. When he finished, the boys wanted more, so our friend sang every song he could think of—in some cases accompanied by the German soldiers—plus a soft-shoe routine. His show over and repertoire exhausted, this Canadian act was escorted by the Germans back over the line where he eventually found the rest of the circus troupe. That's the story of the day!

Rain or no rain, we ended up performing because the covered

grandstand was packed with people waiting for the show to begin. There sat the audience, dry and comfortable, while our emcee walked onstage and into the downpour, collar turned up and rain running down his face, to deliver his welcoming spiel. Dripping wet, yet smiling the whole time, Billy told his jokes and played his harmonica. When finished, our saturated master of ceremonies introduced the Manhattan Models for our A Day at the Beach number. As Jat, with straw hat and cane, merrily sang, we entered one by one, cautiously stepping around in the rain, more intent on staying upright than dancing, and doing our best to avoid any slick metal parts of the stage. Miraculously, it quit raining after that. Fortunately for them, following acts like the Goetsches on the unicycle weren't performing in a deluge, although the stage was certainly still wet and slippery. As luck would have it, the rain started up again just as we were introduced for our last dance routine, the Gypsy. I thought it was pretty funny. Water flew all around as we turned and smacked dripping, rain-soaked tambourines. Got drenched, of course. At least it wasn't cold.

I looked for Mike after the show—after all a bet's a bet—and found him having a beer and bratwurst snack before starting teardown. He seemed surprised to see me. Like yours truly, he was soaking wet. "Well?" I said. "Yeh," he replied, "the Tilt-a-Whirl."

We walked over to the midway. I hadn't noticed before how tall Mike was. He took big steps, and I had trouble keeping up with him. Since my roustabout didn't seem to want to talk, I felt I must be interfering with or interrupting some other plans he had. Still, we'd made a deal and tonight was the payoff! Besides, I considered that this could be the only chance I'd have to be close to him.

Reaching the Tilt-a-Whirl, we found an empty car and stepped aboard. As if in church, Mike and I sat silently while a safety gate and hold-on-for-your-life handlebar snapped shut, locking us into the seat. A bell rang, and the slanted platform beneath our feet lurched into motion, slowly at first, then gradually picking up speed to hurl, spin, lift, and drop us. More than the fun I anticipated of pitching up, down, and sideways while furiously spinning, I looked forward to being thrown against this quiet hunk of male magnetism next to me to check out his green eyes at close range. Well, forget that. I don't think Mike had ever been on a Tilt-a-Whirl before. Poor thing. His head hung down and his eyes rolled, and soon the beer and bratwurst spilled down his chest. The nightmare ride seemed to last forever, and when it was finally over, my dreamboat told me to please go. He said he wanted to sit alone for a minute, so I left him.

Walking back across the fairgrounds alone, I felt embarrassed for Mike and disappointed for myself. Since we're both pretty busy, it's unlikely I'll get to be with Mike again (sigh). But, despite the messy circumstances, I still had fun and still like the Tilt-a-Whirl.

Packed up and left Appleton by about midnight, our usual departure time, but only got two miles out of town when the headlights on the Plymouth faded and died. It was pitch dark, of course. Trying not to panic, Penni carefully turned around and drove slowly, very slowly, back toward Appleton with the three of us hanging out windows, giving directions to keep her on the road. Suddenly we heard a siren, and a car with blinking red lights pulled up behind us. Penni stopped. Seeing two officers get out and come her way, Penni thought for sure they'd give her a ticket. But no, all they did was laugh when they learned they'd stopped a lady with a problem and not some drunken motorist!

Penni followed the police car back to Appleton where the two officers opened up a gas station. They fixed the headlights on the Plymouth, and while they were at it, filled up the gas tank, put in some oil, and checked the speedometer. As we finally drove out of town, Penni waved out the window and honked the horn at our helpers who were locking up again.

Had breakfast in Luverne, Minnesota, at a neat little café that specialized in cinnamon rolls (yum), then continued south.

Now we are in West Point, Nebraska, another flat, dusty, empty town, where it's exceedingly warm and the wind never stops blowing. Checked into the West Point Hotel. There's no matinee today, so we are going to get some rest before tonight's performance.

August 31, 1955

Last night's show was special, as it was our final one. The fair season is over for most of us. Today, many acts are packing up to go back home, wherever that may be. The Bryants will be heading back to Point Pleasant, West Virginia. They didn't sell a lot, I guess, but for them, fairs are simply summer fun and a time to visit with vendors and carnival people they've known in previous fair seasons.

The Manhattan Cocktail Revue, such as it is, stays in West Point until tomorrow, September 1. As yet, we don't know what happens or where we go from here. There's no work, no fairs, no clubs, no nothing. We all hope we can just plain go back home. It's sure been a long time since we've been there.

Yesterday morning, the four of us got downstairs with our luggage. About the time we were checking out, the Herods pulled up and stopped in front of the hotel. While Jat walked around in his cowboy traveling outfit—hat, boots, and all—checking tires, Betty and JoAleene came into the hotel with Cheeka on a leash. They said they were on their way out of town now for the long drive to Point Pleasant, where they'll leave the trailer with the Bryants. Our boss just wanted to tell us goodbye. Then, she cheerfully said, "Go home for a few weeks. Relax and enjoy yourselves. Make up your minds for certain about Europe, and call us as soon as you decide."

Penni went to work packing up the Plymouth. By noon she had the car ready to roll. We were terrifically excited at the prospect of finally going home.

The four of us piled into the Plymouth and headed west out of town. Lori cried a bit and blew her nose a lot, using up my box of Kleenex. I figured she'd perk up once we saw some mountains.

Drove across Nebraska, running into a blizzard, of all things, somewhere around North Platte, that had each of us looking out the car windows to help Penni stay on the road. There were no other cars on the highway going either direction (smart people), and it was pretty dark by then. I got dizzy watching the swirling snowflakes coming at us in the headlights. It seemed like we weren't even moving, but the Plymouth crept along and, thank goodness, did not stall out and die. It seemed an eternity, but we drove out of the snow that gradually turned to rain before stopping altogether.

Crossed into Wyoming and made a breakfast stop in Casper.

Hadn't been there since 1952 when Allene and I barnstormed the West with our dancing teachers, the DeCeciletos, checking every town for clubs, bars, rodeos, jamborees, anything that might need entertainers—and darn near starved. Casper still looks like a busy mining town.

Drove on to Jackson Hole, arriving late, but were able to get rooms at the Utopia Lodge. Got cleaned up and changed then walked over to the Wort Hotel, that special establishment. Noticed they didn't have a floor show, but advertised instead a cowboy band for the Labor Day weekend. Allene asked a couple of people about Dick, but, although his name was familiar, nobody knew his present whereabouts.

It was just over a year ago we were booked into Jackson Hole. None of us had ever heard of it and were astonished at what a charming, little Western town it was. We did three shows nightly at the Wort Hotel in the main room, while The Whispering Winds and Sons of the Golden West alternated music sets to entertain patrons in the adjacent Silver Dollar Bar. This is where we met Dick.

There was a small casino in a room next to the Silver Dollar Bar where Dick liked to play blackjack every night. I don't think he was much of a gambler. But he was a nice, likable fellow and made friends easily. I remember Dick loved the outdoors, and during the day he took my sister and me on hikes around Jackson Hole, which was his favorite place in the whole wide world. Checked out Snow King Mountain, Jenny Lake, and Jackson Lake with our lovable guide. Dick was indeed a charmer, and we were with him every day. He'd take us to breakfast each night after work too, giving both of us a kiss on the cheek when he brought us back to our motel. Like all the others, though, Dick had his eye on Allene. Her smile gets them every time. Of course, she's more interesting too.

September 4, 1955

Checked out of the Utopia Lodge yesterday morning and drove to where Dick's hot dog stand was located on the highway going north. It was closed and had a "for sale" sign taped over the front window. The whole area looked overgrown like the property had not been used in some time. Allene got out of the car and just stared at it awhile. Penni offered to hang around another day if my sister wanted to do some inquiring. Allene just shook her head.

It was about noon when we drove out of Jackson Hole and up to Yellowstone to see if Old Faithful was still doing its thing. We continued driving west, across Montana and into Idaho. Seeing all the forests and mountains made each of us more anxious than ever to get to the coast. It's been over a year since Penni, Allene, and I left. Stopped at the Sillman Hotel in Spokane, Washington, for the night.

The last time Allene and I stayed in Spokane, we were trying to get Dave Sobel, one of the biggest agents in the West, to book us. Sobel did get us a job in Kennewick down near the Oregon border at the Kennewick Social Club where the club manager took one look at our teenage, makeup-free faces and flew into a rage! He ordered us to stay out of his club except to perform, so we hid every night between shows in the supply room, where we changed. Couldn't wait to finish *that* job.

September 5, 1955

Arrived in Seattle yesterday by way of Snoqualmie Pass. Boy, did those miles and miles of evergreens look great! Penni dropped Allene and me off at the President Hotel downtown, a place we've stayed many times because of the neat, clean rooms with kitchens and nearness to the city center. The desk clerk remembered us and the Manhattan Cocktail Revue from two years ago. Got checked in then called Mom to let her know we were close and coming home!

Today, Allene and I took the train headed to Vancouver, BC, an old familiar run for us. Every time we played the Seattle area and had time off, we took this train as far as Mt. Vernon, where Papa met and drove us home to Anacortes. Usually, we stayed only a few days and then traveled back to Seattle to meet the Herods and go to our next booking. But this time, for sure, we'll be staying in Anacortes for several weeks, since future plans are uncertain.

This afternoon, Papa met Allene and me at the train station in Mt. Vernon, as before. He had to gaze at us for a moment, like making sure we were really his girls. Papa looks the same—grey haired and balding, bespectacled and rosy faced in his plaid flannel shirt with drab, heavy denim trousers held up by green suspenders. I know Papa's glad we're back, but as usual, he didn't actually say so. Instead, he started right off talking about progress on the house and yard as he drove home to Anacortes and the refurbished house on 38th Street that Allene and I had never seen.

Upon arrival, Mom rushed out to greet us with a surprised look on her face, as though she wasn't expecting anyone! Her hair was pulled into a tight bun, and she wore the pink, flowered dress she bought to go to Easter services years ago. She wiped her hands on her apron, then gave us each a big hug and helped get our bags into a little bedroom off the kitchen. She talked so much and asked so many questions she almost forgot the chicken frying on the stove!

Got moved in and then enjoyed Mom's fried chicken dinner with mashed potatoes, corn, and lemon meringue pie. Boy, I have a feeling Allene and I will gain weight if we stay very long! Talked a lot at dinner, heard about friends and relatives, and got to bed late. Tired as I was, I couldn't get to sleep. Been a long time getting here.

September 8, 1955

Yesterday, Allene baked cookies to send to Kent Porter and the boys. After that, she wrote letters to Dick, Jim, Ray, Cal, Don, and Francis. She doesn't talk about Dick or what could have happened. Apparently, he's getting her letters since none were returned, so he is indeed in Jackson Hole. Big question: why isn't he writing?

Mom and Papa's house is wonderful with a kind of woodsy smell in the front part where the fireplace is. Except for the bedrooms, there are no doors—which makes the place seem bigger. It's not quite finished, but cute, like a bungalow or cabin. And the view across Anacortes to Guemes and Cypress Islands is fabulous! The town below looks like a relief map—city blocks like squares on a board and houses that resemble those used in Monopoly, with patches of green for yards, front and back. Then, of course, miniature toy cars come and go on the strips between the squares. Ha! And once in a while a ship sails down or up Guemes Channel. It's easy to just stand gazing out that front window all day instead of getting anything done.

On the days Mom clerks at Penney's, Papa drives her to and from because we're a couple of miles from downtown, and Anacortes still doesn't have a bus service. Mom never did learn to drive. Anyway, Allene does the cooking if Mom has to work, plus keeps the kitchen clean. She likes to do that kind of stuff. Also, my sister plans to make curtains for all the windows in the house before we have to leave again—if we ever do.

It's nice to be back home and just doing nothing in particular. Yesterday, I went through boxes of stuff Allene and I had sent home, pasting souvenirs, news clippings, show flyers, and photos in scrapbooks. That took some time. What didn't make it into a scrapbook got put back into a box and marked for contents and date. After that, I went outside to help Papa in the yard. While I was moving rocks in the wheelbarrow, I noticed two skunks watching me. As soon as I turned their way, they beat it fast into the woods. So cute!

Tonight at dinner, the subject of going to Europe got kicked around some. Papa still thinks it's too far and anything can happen. In some of those foreign places, people can just plain disappear, he said, and he should know, having sailed all over the world on ships in the Merchant Marine since he was twelve. We ought to stay in Anacortes, he continued, and get used to "normal" living, then perhaps go to Seattle for better job opportunities.

Mom didn't like that idea. She wants us to stay in show business, not traveling around so much, but appearing on television shows. Seems like everyone (except our family) is getting TV sets now, she commented. It's the latest thing. All a person hears about in Anacortes is what's on television. As far as going overseas, she thought it would be nice to see other countries, but they're "behind the times" if you're trying to find jobs and get anywhere. And don't forget the language barrier, she concluded. These are all good things to consider, I guess. Anyway, lots to think about. Helped with dishes then went to bed.

September 12, 1955

Yesterday, Mom had the day off. The weather was good, so we packed a lunch and took the ferry over to Guemes Island. Papa drove across to North Beach, one of our favorite places, where we enjoyed slowly walking along the shore looking for agates. Anyway, we discovered the beach was deserted, and the tide was out. Strolled along observing little crabs scurrying between the wet rocks and kelp, sand fleas hopping, and starfish clinging to the undersides of boulders. Mom and Papa didn't walk very far. They sat on a log waiting while Allene and I trekked off toward West Beach, promising to be back in an hour.

At first, Allene and I did nothing but step across logs or jump over rocks in silence. Soon, different islands came into view, so we'd definitely turned a corner, so to speak. Keeping her pace, my sister suddenly blurted out that she thinks Dick has a girlfriend or may even be married, and if he doesn't answer her latest letter, that's that. She hadn't really cared in the first place, she said. After all, what did she actually know about him? Well, in any case, what happens, happens for the best, Allene snapped in summation. But there was more.

My sister slowed down. She said that by the time we arrive in Great Britain in October, we'll definitely need the mouton jackets presently in storage, plus some wool slacks and heavy sweaters. We'll need city maps and good solid shoes for "hoofing it" around London, and, because it will be the theater season, the two of us should check out the shows as soon as we get settled in a nice downtown hotel. Allene thought it was a good idea to stay in Europe for a year, and, while on the Continent, to learn songs in other languages for our act. If we have the time, the Halliday Twins will explore world capitals—maybe even meet millionaires—and become ultra-cosmopolitan because of exposure to many cultures. And just think of the grand old buildings, cathedrals, and museums! All that history and good things to learn about everywhere we travel. And we won't be alone. The Herods will be there. Penni's going, and Lori is too.

Returned to Mom and Papa sitting on the log, sifting through pebbles looking for agates. Neither seemed surprised or upset when Allene told them we had more or less decided to go overseas for one year. Mom said because of the dampness in England, we should take along some warm cotton underwear that reaches to the knees (aka "huggies"). And we must see Buckingham Palace, the Changing of the Guard, and the Tower of London. Papa didn't say anything.

As luck would have it, Betty called from West Virginia that evening to let us know the revue opens in Louisville at the Iroquois Gardens on September 19 for two weeks. From there, we go to Nashville for another two-week engagement. Great! Allene told Betty that she and I will sail to England with them a month from now, and our boss seemed relieved. We must get passport pictures and boat tickets as soon as possible if we intend to sail aboard the *Île de France*, leaving on October 19 from New York.

This morning, sensing the urgency of moving ahead with the plan, Allene and I had Papa drive us to Mt. Vernon where we caught the train for Seattle. Spent the day in the city getting our passport pictures and reserving the boat tickets from a steamship agency. Since we'll be leaving this area soon, the pictures and tickets will be sent to Anacortes where Mom will need to forward them to Louisville. So far so good.

September 19, 1955

Left Anacortes four days ago. It was pouring rain as Mom, Papa, Allene, and I went over to Mt. Vernon in the Buick for the last time. As always, Mom packed a lunch of fruit and cold chicken for our trip. This time, though, she also gave us $400 survival money, just in case. Hated to take it, but since we don't know what lies ahead, Allene reluctantly stuck the bills in her purse.

After giving Mom and Papa each a long hug and a kiss, Allene and I boarded the train for Seattle, like we've done so many times before. Waved goodbye through the train window, but Mom and Papa didn't see me. Watching the wrong passenger car for a last glimpse, they missed seeing us altogether as the train chugged forward. Wonder when we'll see them again.

Spent the night at the President Hotel in Seattle and had breakfast at Clark's Round the Clock the next morning. Then, to save money, Allene and I hauled our luggage onto a city bus and got off at the King Street Station. Penni and Lori were already there saying farewell to their parents and promising to send postcards home. They kissed and hugged before turning around and joining

Allene and me to board the train.

Aboard the Empire Builder, we took our seats and settled in. We had coach seats, so knew we'd be sleeping sitting up for the next couple of nights. Thank goodness the seats were soft and comfortable.

The first part of the trip was through the Cascades. The four of us hurried to the Vista Dome car to see the trees, mountains, and rushing streams we'd missed for over a year. Soon enough they were gone, slipping by us as the train sped on to Grand Coulee country and sagebrush.

After leaving Spokane, we traveled east across the top of Idaho and into Montana. By now it was night, but I didn't sleep well. Kept waking up to peer out the window at whatever I could see rushing by, like shimmering lakes or silhouetted mountains. At daybreak, we put our watches ahead because the porter said we'd crossed into another time zone. Saw lots of flat, open land looking white and icy already. By dinnertime, the train was in North Dakota.

Allene and I joined Penni and Lori in the diner and heard what a great time they'd had in Seattle going places with their friends. But, like us, they said they'd eaten too much during the entire stay. Penni found it hard to leave the old green Plymouth behind. But she is looking forward to seeing the famous continental attractions, because her aunt gave her a guide to European travel as a going away gift.

On the third day out, we woke up in Minneapolis and went lickety-split from there to Union Station in Chicago, arriving in the dark. We needed to change stations to catch a train going south. This second train, owned by a different line, smelled musty and seemed to be running on square wheels!

We endured a very bumpy ride all the way from Chicago to Louisville, arriving the next morning tired out, only to find our luggage hadn't come with us. Took a taxi to the Hermitage Hotel, where we'd stayed last January. The Herods were already checked in. They'd left the station wagon and trailer in West Virginia. Now none of us has transportation and will need to take taxis everywhere.

Went to rehearsal at the club in the afternoon and were amazed to find out Kent Porter's Band is going to play the show! Sure will be good to see them again.

The Iroquois Gardens was jam-packed for our opening tonight, and since our bags still weren't here, the four of us had to wear the same slacks and sweaters to the club we'd lived in on the train. Fortunately, the Herods didn't have luggage delays, so we had music and costumes for our shows.

It's so funny, we are still bobbing from the trip and can't even brush our teeth in front of a mirror without swaying from side to side!

Manhattan Models, Hilltop Casino, East Dubuque, Illinois.
Pat and Penni in front, Allene and Lori standing, 1955.

Chapter Sixteen

September 22, 1955

Every night, crowds at the club have been big and boisterous. Found out there's a convention in Louisville, so that's why we're seeing all the party people. Mainly, because of our boss, the revue's going over really well. To be sure, Kent's group gets all the cues and tempos correct, but Jat plays his violin throughout most of the show. It's extra work for him but worth it, as our music is so important. I'm sure Kent doesn't mind being musically prodded and pulled by our boss. He almost idolizes the Herods.

Mr. Gould came to town yesterday and seemed very glad to see us again. The first thing he did was get our luggage picked up and brought to the hotel. According to the baggage attendant, the bags were put by mistake on a train for Atlanta that got delayed and rerouted when a bridge collapsed near Knoxville. Good story! Well, at least we've got our clothes. Boy, was it neat to wear a cocktail dress again. Mr. Gould came out to the Iroquois Gardens to see the revue and to buy steak, orchids, and champagne between shows. Since we were leaving the country, he gave each of us chocolates and a silk scarf as going-away gifts. Such a nice person.

Today, bright and early, JoAleene knocked on our hotel room door. Mr. Gould, she said, was in the hotel lobby, waiting to say goodbye to everyone. The Herods felt we all owed him a kiss on the cheek for all he'd done for the show. After delivering her message,

JoAleene rushed off.

Penni and the Herods were already in the lobby, shaking hands and saying goodbye to Mr. Gould when Allene and I got there. Standing on either side of him, my sister and I dutifully bestowed a hug and a kiss on our generous friend from Chicago. He beamed rosily from ear to ear. We were in for a wonderful adventure, he said, pulling us close, so, no matter what happens, make the most of living abroad. Then, with a wave and a smile, he ducked into a cab and was gone.

September 25, 1955

Yesterday, Joann called Penni to say she had taken a Greyhound bus all the way from Anderson, Indiana, to wish us a *bon voyage*, and would appreciate it if someone could pick her up at the depot! Luckily, Kent stopped by the Hermitage, so Penni grabbed him to drive her to the bus station.

Joann moved in with Penni and Lori. After she'd unpacked, we sat around and talked and talked about Peg and Red, our leaving the USA, Frank, Kent, and Joann's new boyfriend. His name is Joe, and it sounds like they're getting serious.

Dressed and put on our makeup early so Penni, Lori, Joann, Allene, and I could have dinner at the club before the first show. We treated Joann, because she had made the effort to see us, and it might be a while before we're all together again. The Herods stopped by to say hello. Then, during the first show, our boss played Joann's favorite songs on the violin, serenading her at the table. Nice. There she was in the spotlight and looking really pleased.

Next came the real shock of the day. Between shows, Betty announced that the Chicago agent called earlier. Unfortunately, our Nashville booking has fallen through because the labor union shut down the club. That means we'll be out of work next week. All of us were really counting on that salary.

September 27, 1955

Yesterday afternoon, Joann had to leave. Penni, Lori, Allene, and I said goodbye and promised to send our Hoosier friend a postcard every week and some French perfume if we get to Paris. Kent took a bunch of goofy glamour girl snapshots of the five of us together, then he and Penni delivered Joann to the bus depot. By now, I guess she is back home in Anderson, Indiana.

Later, Kent took Penni out for dinner at his favorite Italian restaurant. From there they caught a movie at one of the big downtown movie theaters. Denny called Allene earlier to see if they could make the dinner/movie date a foursome, but my sister declined. Today, Betty came by the hotel room to report that Jat had called the London agent and been informed regarding a four-month USO tour of bases around the Mediterranean. The money would be good, but travel arrangements, accommodations, and regular meals would be iffy at best, with no guarantees. For the North African countries, we'd need cholera, typhus, typhoid, and who-knows-what-else shots. Also, we would be traveling by bus from site to site most of the time. Wonderful.

Frowning and beginning to pace, Betty said that JoAleene and Cheekaboom could not come on the USO tour with us. No children, no pets, even if you pay for them. Military regulations. Also, the minimum age is eighteen, she added, so yours truly just eked by as far as being eligible to play this safari circuit. The tour begins in England, so filling out forms to get work permits would be necessary and must be seen to immediately—if the Herods decide to book it.

Allene and I broke in our new, revised Sisters routine last night, singing the Irving Berlin hit song. The first chorus is straightforward, with lyrics about friendly sisters. Then, the second chorus, with special lyrics written by Jat, does a switcheroo, where the sisters snarl at one another. It's kind of long, so there's lots to remember. And, as usual, although Betty's gestures are cute, we move around so much that it's difficult to stay close to the microphone. Can't just stand still to sing, I guess.

Today, I started on the new, green costumes with lots of beads that Betty designed earlier. My poor eyeballs! We're sewing silver bugle beads in a serpentine pattern on lime-green crepe breakaway dresses. The bodice has a low-cut top and draped peplum at the bottom, making the most of the soft, smooth fabric. Tucking under the peplum, the skirt is straight and will be attached with snaps. Should look great, but all that bead sewing takes beaucoup time for both of us.

Apparently, the revue is going to be out of work for two weeks when we close here. Last night, Jat mentioned that he has tried but can't get a booking on short notice anywhere. Maybe we'll end up going to Joann's, but I don't know how we'll get there with no car. None of us is anxious to spend extra money on transportation—or anything else!

October 1, 1955

Gave Jat a belated birthday party at the club last night, because we were on the West Coast when it was his actual birthday. Penni, Lori, Allene, and I went together and bought him some concert-type records he's been wanting. The celebration between shows was a real surprise for Jat. Waiters brought out a chocolate cake topped with white frosting, decorated with a music staff and different instruments in various colors. Kent and the boys played "Happy Birthday" when it was delivered to the party table, and the whole audience joined in singing. Kind of neat.

Today, our passports finally arrived. Got a little excited and queasy at the prospect of what might lie ahead. Adventure? Starvation? Scary when there are no definite bookings yet. Now that we actually have our passports, all the talking about going overseas is over. It's for certain we're leaving—and with only one-way boat tickets! Allene says the best part of going to Europe will be coming back. I think Mom and Papa feel the same way but would never say so.

The Herods rented a projector this afternoon, hung a sheet up on the wall of their hotel room, and had a party to show their home movies of England, Scotland, and France taken earlier this year. Kent, Denny, and the rest of the band came with bags of popcorn, Hershey's Kisses, and 7 Up. Too bad most of the film was either overexposed, jittery, or totally black. I'm afraid we didn't see much of England, Scotland, and France. Had a good time, though, laughing and eating and trying to imagine what we were missing.

Leaving the hotel to catch a cab for work tonight, Allene and I saw Ish Kabibble checking into the Hermitage. He looked just the same as when he performed with the Kay Kyser show during the war, wearing the loud suit and sporting his soup-bowl haircut. Had to stop and get his autograph. He said he's opening soon at the Merry-Go-Round club in Louisville (our competition), so we'll have to catch his act.

This was our closing night at the Iroquois Gardens, and what a finish it was! Mac, the owner, popped a bottle of champagne and gave a toast to the future of the revue. He's known the Herods and booked the revue yearly (at least) since about 1950. It seemed a good time to talk about those days passed, when the Manhattan Cocktail Revue drew a crowd to see their complete variety show with glamourous dancers, lots of music, and laughs. As Mac said, it was a solid, fast-paced entertainment package described as "a little Las Vegas" or "the well-mixed comedy cocktail" or "a last glimpse of vaudeville." And here we are out of work until further notice. Super.

Jat is going ahead with the four-month air force contract and work permits for England. Something needs to be resolved concerning JoAleene and Cheekaboom, but, Betty said, they'd cross that bridge when they come to it.

I spent the afternoon sewing silver beads on the new costume—should be gorgeous if it's ever finished—while Allene went for a drive with Denny to see the fall colors outside Louisville. It was a sunny day with a blue sky and all, so I guess the trees looked their finest. I could have gone too. But, since Denny's been asking my sister out and always getting turned down, I thought I'd best stay put. Besides, one of us needs to be sewing beads every day.

When she and Denny came back after a couple of hours, Allene and I walked over to the Blue Boar for dinner. The Herods were there, so after eating, the five of us took a cab to the Merry-Go-Round, where our new friend Ish Kabibble is performing. Although there were line dancers and a stripper, Ish did most of the show himself and was very funny, telling down-home-on-the-farm stories and finishing with some rousing horn playing. It's too bad the club is so darn small and smoky. A person has to sit practically knee to knee with other patrons, looking up at a cluttered little stage. The lighting isn't real good either. The show ran continuously, and in case anyone got bored, they could watch a television show in progress on a giant set near the bar! With so much going on, I think the place should be called Three Ring Circus instead of the Merry-Go-Round.

October 8, 1955

This morning, the Herods left for Point Pleasant, where they'll stay with the Bryants during our week's layoff. Penni and Lori took a bus up to visit Joann. Allene and I plan to remain here at the Hermitage until they all return, sewing beads or watching free television in the hotel lobby. Before leaving, the Herods suggested Allene and I stash $500 somewhere as reserve money, in case we need boat fare to get back to the States! I imagine they told Penni and Lori to do the same. That's pretty good considering we haven't even left yet.

Allene decided we have too many clothes for overseas travel, so we're sending a suitcase home. For sure, we won't need a bunch of cocktail dresses and high heels on the military tour. On the other hand, we can use our fur jackets in cold, damp England. Therefore, we must contact Dee at the furrier in Dubuque to ship them down pronto. (Forgot to do that earlier.) So we won't miss anything, I think we need to buy a movie camera for traveling in Europe, but Allene says we better stick to simple essentials such as a hot water bottle, boots, and big purses with shoulder straps. We'll check out Grants for that stuff.

If we ever run out of beads, we have another project to keep us busy. Betty thinks we should get some blank charts and India ink to make a backup set of our musical arrangements. Maybe we can get Kent to proofread what we turn out to be certain we get the symbols correct and make them legible. His band is still out at the Iroquois Gardens but is closing soon. Their next job is Cairo, Illinois.

October 13, 1955

Checked out of the Hermitage on the eleventh and left Louisville with Kent, who managed to book the Halliday Twins for a split week at Club Charming in Cairo with his band. What a guy!

No sooner had we begun the trip to Illinois when Kent's car sputtered and died in a little town called Leitchfield, only about sixty miles from Louisville. Since it was evening, no vehicle repair places were open. Kent fussed and fumed. I think knowing little about cars and fearing the worst, Kent thought he might have to buy a new one! Not just that. Always concerned and caring, the band leader wanted to arrive early in Cairo, so he could do several rehearsals to be sure the music was right. Instead, we were delayed in a little town that might not have the parts or expertise to get us rolling again anytime soon.

Had to stay overnight at the hotel in Leitchfield and hope a mechanic would be available at some local garage in the morning. If Denny had been with us, he might have known what was wrong with Kent's buggy, but he had gone on ahead to Cairo. Our tough luck!

After just a few hours' sleep and before breakfast, the three of us beat it over to a maintenance and body shop, where we planted ourselves in front of the garage doors, waiting for the place to open. Thanks to some really nice, friendly people who found the problem right away, we roared out of Leitchfield in just a couple of hours, equipped with a new fuel pump. Kent appeared truly relieved it wasn't anything worse. After arriving later that day in Cairo, Allene and I checked into our reserved apartment run by Club Charming's owner, Becky. Wonderful.

This morning, we ate breakfast at a place called the Keller Coffee Shop, not far from where we're staying. Good poached eggs. How I appreciate that! Walked around the town afterward. Cairo's like an interesting old settlement, not very large but with lots of bars and clubs in dingy buildings that look about one hundred years old and kind of soggy, probably because the Mississippi River surrounds the whole place.

Since the club is located miles out on the outskirts of Cairo, Allene and I took a cab to rehearsal in the afternoon. Unfortunately, the band has never played our music before, so we had to run through it again and again. Pretty darn tiring, but Allene and I feel lucky to have a three-day booking fall into our laps. Makes us appreciate Kent all the more.

We opened tonight, and although Club Charming's not a classy place, they sure pack in a terrific audience. After our act, Allene and

I took bow after bow and felt like stars! In addition, Becky wants to have us back for a longer engagement sometime. (That's a nice boost for our not-so-confident egos!) We do three shows a night, working with a male singer/emcee, a stripper, and a line of girls. Actually, there's something happening onstage continuously from the time the club opens. A second band fills in time, as needed, between acts in addition to Kent's group with Denny's goofy antics, like marching over the piano to liven things up! Terrific.

Adding to the thrill and excitement of opening night, a fight broke out. Kent and the boys had just left the bandstand when, clear back in the dressing room, we could hear glasses smashing as tables and chairs went over in the club with guys yelling and women screaming! Extra pronto, the Cairo Police were on the scene, bursting through both front and back doors. I don't think anyone was arrested, but all kinds of people were milling around inside and outside the club. A few minutes later, the second band hurried onstage, and the normal entertainment resumed.

Later, Kent told us that just before fists started flying, someone had yelled out a request for "The Great Speckled Bird." Can't help but wonder if this was the same guy who was thrown out of the Club Paramount in Albany! Anyway, Kent yelled back that he didn't know the song and launched into something else—and all hell broke loose!

October 16, 1955

Last night, the club was a packed house for our closing. Many in the audience were return customers, so I guess they really dug the Club Charming's big, continuous show. By the applause we got, Allene and I knew we were THE headliners. Such a nice change to be loved and in demand! Between performances, we went around the club talking and drinking champagne with our fans, making the most of our temporary celebrity status. Met a Mr. Halliday who thought we might be related. Guess there is even a park in Cairo named after this old family. Have to write Papa about this.

Following our final show, Denny hosted a farewell party with champagne and barbecued ribs for everyone involved. While I thoroughly enjoyed the feast, I got to thinking about the expense. It must have cost Denny a bundle. I think he played the big spender to impress my sister. Afterward, he tried to persuade Allene to go back to Louisville with him in his car, but Kent intervened, reminding Denny that *he* was chauffeuring the twins.

Today, we were up and packed by noon, and had nothing to do but wait for our favorite band leader to pick us up. Kent arrived and we left soggy, old Cairo and its great audiences. Since the band is booked for another two weeks at the Iroquois Gardens, driving us back to Louisville is not out of Kent's way. I think they go to Shreveport next. Our "chauffeur" seemed so happy and enthusiastic, telling us about himself: how he'd entered college and become a psychology major, how he'd dropped out and gone into acting, only to quit because he couldn't stand New York City. Fortunately, Kent always loved all kinds of music, so he became a piano player. Then, he had a heart attack and needed to redesign his life, but not dramatically.

He went on about Allene and me, saying he'd decided when he met us that we were not twins. No one had ever doubted us before, as far as I know. No matter. Of course, the longer Kent knew us, the more convinced he became that our pretense amounted to some silly show biz gimmick. And if it works, better make the most of it. Anyway, he wants to build a revue of his own—like the Herods— and would love having the Halliday Twins in it. There'd be singing, dancing, comedy skits, and, in time, more dancers or acts would join, providing greater variety. Or something like that. He was aware that we were going to leave the country because it was so hard to find enough work here to keep our revue booked. Still, it was his dream, and he wanted to give it a try.

The band leader was disappointed about Penni. Somehow he'd misread her from the beginning, he reflected, but enjoyed the times they'd spent together. He thought a bit. "We are like children," he slowly began, "taking chances because of a need to learn, then can't stop learning even when knowing more sometimes hurts." Our friend didn't have any more to say after that, so the three of us pretty much just watched the road ahead for the rest of the trip.

Kent dropped us off at the Hermitage Hotel, and we said goodbye. Feeling a pang of regret, I wondered if I'd ever see him again. Allene and I walked through the revolving door and into the lobby with our bags. Were surprised to see the Herods at the registration desk. Jat, Betty, and JoAleene appeared a bit tuckered from traveling, but perked right up when Allene told them about our Cairo booking and our great success with the act. Couldn't talk long because of the packing we still had to do. We're down to the wire now! Fortunately, our furs arrived from storage in Dubuque and were held here by the hotel manager.

October 19, 1955

After hardly sleeping a wink, Allene and I were up at the crack of dawn on the seventeenth. We were so excited about going to New York that we practically ran into one another getting our bags into the lobby. Checked out of the hotel, and got a cab to the bus station, where Allene and I boarded the first Greyhound of the day heading northeast. The Herods planned to take a later bus, but Allene and I wanted to have time to sightsee in the famous metropolis, so went on ahead. The whole journey from Louisville to New York City lasted twenty-four hours. We had to change buses twice. Since we slept most of the way, the trip wasn't bad. Because the driver made many stops, we were able to run out and grab something to eat or find a bathroom, then get back on the bus and sleep some more.

Arrived in New York City on the morning of the eighteenth, took a cab to the Mansfield Hotel, got checked in, then set out to see as many attractions as we could. Did a lot of strolling and gawking, mostly up at skyscrapers. Plenty of traffic, noise, and one heck of a lot of concrete everywhere. If I had to live in New York City, I think I'd get tired of all the hard grey slab real quick.

Late in the afternoon, while we were walking along Broadway wondering where to eat dinner, something really surprising happened. Of all things, we ran smack into someone we knew. It was Lou Mosconi, a performer from our Seattle days when Allene and I danced in the chorus at the Showbox. He was just as amazed as we were and insisted on taking us home with him to New Jersey for dinner. It was all Allene and I could do to keep up with Lou in the commuter crowd in the subway station. When we arrived in New

Jersey at the trailer park where Lou and his wife, Camille, lived, the power was out. Camille's pork roast lay cold and raw in the oven, so we sat around eating peanut butter sandwiches and talking about Seattle, Hollywood, New York, and show business, but mostly how hard it was to get bookings these days. Apparently, Lou and Camille had been in New York for months and not getting anywhere. In fact, Camille had taken a modeling job to pay the bills.

The Herods are smart to leave the country, Lou remarked, and we're lucky to get to go with them. "So you're taking a chance," he said. "What the hell? There's nothing much here anymore." He wished he and Camille could go too, but they haven't the funds right now. Dismal.

After saying goodbye and good luck to the Mosconis, Allene and I caught the subway back to Manhattan, where we stopped by a theater box office and tried to get tickets to Lerner and Loewe's musical *My Fair Lady* for tonight. Sold out—for months. Returned to the Mansfield and just went to bed. We were bushed anyway. Later, when Penni and Lori had checked in, we chatted with them about their visit to Joann's when we were working in Cairo. They met Joe and confirmed he is nice and very good looking. He and Joann are planning to be married.

Took a cab to the French Line this morning, expecting to meet up with the Herods checking in. Because the dock was a milling madhouse of people, luggage, taxis, porters, you name it, the four of us had to keep moving or get run over. Searched and searched but couldn't find the Herods anywhere in the crowd. Without a word, men in blue uniforms swiftly scooped up our luggage and away it went—to our cabins, we hoped.

Sailing time approached and still no Herods. Penni and Allene went to watch all the incoming cabs, while Lori and I scanned the counters in the boarding area. Beginning to feel sick with worry, I suddenly spotted JoAleene waving a French flag and shouting as she pushed her way toward me. Her parents were taking care of arrangements for Cheekaboom on the ship. We're going tourist class, but the little dog has to travel first class! Lucky dog.

Finally, we all managed to get together and walked up the

gangplank onto the French Line's *Île de France*, our home for the next week. Betty said not to look for our cabin just yet. Since we'll be performing en route, our tourist class accommodations will be changed to cabin class, as a way of paying us for entertaining the passengers. So we'll get moved in a couple of hours. Nice.

With extra time and nothing else to do anyway, Penni, Lori, Allene, and I strolled the promenade deck and peeked into the passageways and big salons. Travelers, bellboys, floral bouquets, luggage, and visitors blocked the ship's lobbies and aisles leading to the other side of the vessel. That was okay. We were content to walk along the deck gazing at the New York skyline and the Statue of Liberty. Great sights.

Soon, however, a man with a camera approached Allene and me. He flashed a press card, saying he was from the *New York Times*, and asked if we would mind if he took photos of us to advertise the French Line. Arrivals and departures of international travelers are of interest to a readership not so privileged, he remarked. Ha! Allene answered, "Why not?" and told the photographer we were in a revue that would perform for the passengers during the crossing. He said he'd guessed as much. With our furs, figures, and blonde hair, we were obviously in show business. After snapping a series of "cheesecake" shots he added that we looked like a sister act.

Anyway, this fellow envied us our voyage, saying that going to Europe was something he'd wanted to do for the experience, but he'd gotten married instead. He observed that those countries might not have American luxuries, but when you're young, you manage. You also make the most of where you are. To finish his roll of film, he had Allene and me climb into a lifeboat and wave goodbye to the Statue of Liberty while hanging onto a lifesaving ring.

It did seem fitting.

The End

Mon. – Sept. 14 – Sent a $1 38 money order to
Dee to finish payments on our stoles. We
hope to get them while we're in Dallas.
We had a dress rehearsal for Merry Widow
& practiced getting out of the dress & hat
then rushed home, ate, fixed our hair
& got back in time for band rehearsal.
We served wardrobe until showtime
& up until it was time to go on
in the Merry Widow. The number
went very well & we all held our
splits. Joan's leg must have hurt
her too, because she was crying
when she came off. We got a postcard
from Mr. & Mrs. Klein in East Dubuque.
Jo Aleene fell asleep on our couch, so
the Herods decided maybe they'd
better let her spend the night with
us.

Tues. Sept. 15 – Jo Aleene went to her catechism & Pat &
went down to the club & practiced Merry W.,
toe & some of the old dances like mambo,
cakewalk, etc. We wrote a short letter to
Mom, but we haven't heard from her in
quite a little while. We read our respective
books as we ate dinner. I'm reading

Epilogue

Pat and her sister Allene continued performing to enthusiastic audiences into the 1990s on cruise ships, at conventions, benefits, senior centers, and retirement homes.

New York City skyline in October 1955 from the deck of the French oceanliner Ile de France.

Other titles in this series

Fifties Kids by Allene Halliday (©2019)

Here Comes the Showboat by Betty Bryant (©1994)

Acknowledgements

Sincere appreciation to the crew at
The Print Guys/B&B Printing in Kennewick, Washington,
for all their help.

Special thanks to Chloe Hovind and Jessica Moreland in the
Village Books Publishing Department in Bellingham, Washington,
for project management assistance.

Additional thanks to the following people:

Bob and Tina Lagonegro
Sean and Manal Lagonegro
Corey Babarovich
Todd Babarovich

Many thanks to Peter Lagonegro and Maddie Grant for their
technical assistance.

www.ingramcontent.com/pod-product-compliance
Lightning Source LLC
Chambersburg PA
CBHW051102050726
47592CB00002B/638